LIGHTEST BLUES
Great Humor from the Thirties

TEXT BY
Jane Van Nimmen

EDITED BY
Clive Giboire

IMAGO IMPRINT INC.   NEW YORK CITY

IMAGO IMPRINT INC.
150 Fifth Avenue, New York, N.Y. 10011

Editor-in-Chief: Clive Giboire
Creative Director: Arnold Skolnick
Associate Editor: Claire Johnson
Assistant Editor: Suzanne Gagné
Art Associate: Elizabeth Kodela
Production: Karen Fox
Typography: Larry Lorber, Ultracomp

Imago Books are distributed by
Horizon Press
156 Fifth Avenue, New York, N.Y. 10010

Library of Congress Cataloging in Publication Data

Van Nimmen, Jane, 1937-
   Lightest Blues.

   "Selections from Americana magazine, 1932-33."
   Bibliography: p.
   Includes index.
   1. American wit and humor.   2. American wit and
humor,
Pictorial.   I. Giboire, Clive.   II. Title.
PN6161.V328   1984   817'.52'08   84-9065
ISBN 0-915829-51-7
ISBN 0-915829-52-5 (pbk.)

10 9 8 7 6 5 4 3 2 1
Printed in the United States of America

To the memory of

"Alexander King, because as the Vienna-born and
Manhattan-bred editor of that vitriolic and
Rabelaisian broadside, *Americana*, he fears neither
God nor Mammon and frequently invites the wrath
of both; because at thirty-three he has produced full
sets of illustrations for thirty books, from Congreve
to O'Neill; and because he uses a battery of pseudonyms to cover up the fact that he translates Roman
classics, draws dramatic cartoons, concocts satirical
manifestoes, and writes serious essays for a
mystified public."

Nomination for the Hall of Fame
Vanity Fair, August 1933

and to

the audacious spirit of the *Americana* contributors.

ACKNOWLEDGEMENT

We are particularly indebted to Margie Barab, Robert
and Edith Disraeli, Peter and Martin Grosz, Perkins
Harnly, Al and Dolly Hirschfeld, Sylvia Lazarus, William
Steig, and May and Lynd Ward for their generosity in
consenting to interviews and correspondence that stirred
both joyful and painful memories. We are also grateful to
Nora Hodges and Loren MacIver for their recollections of
Americana contributors. Special thanks are due the
Library of Congress, where the Rare Books and the
Research Facilities Divisions substantially aided our
undertaking. Bernard Reilly of the Library's Prints and
Photographs Division was especially helpful. George
Barringer, chief of Special Collections in the Lauinger
Library, Georgetown University, kindly made available
the Lynd Ward archives. We received additional guidance
from Steven Heller, Elizabeth Gilmore Holt, Milton
Kaplan, Barbara Shissler Nosanow, and Judith
O'Sullivan. We are grateful to Mr. and Mrs. Lynd Ward
for permission to reproduce two Ward wood engravings,
Self-Portrait (1929) and *Portrait of Art Young;* to Peggy
Bacon for permission to reproduce her caricature self-
portrait from *Off With Their Heads* (1934); to the
Houghton Library, Harvard University, and to the estate
of E.E. Cummings for permission to reproduce two
illustrations from *CIOPW* (1932) copyright © 1931, 1959 by
E.E. Cummings; and to Condé Nast for permission to
reprint Alexander King's "The Sad Case of the Humorous
Magazines," which appeared in the December 1933 issue of
Vanity Fair, copyright © 1933 (renewed) 1961 by The
Condé Nast Publications Inc.; and to the estate of
S.J. Perelman for permission to reprint *Scenario* which
appeared in the February 1932 issue of *Contact*.

TABLE OF CONTENTS

EDITOR'S NOTE

Many of the articles from *Americana* are facsimiles of the original typography.

William Steig, cover for *Americana*, December 1932

INTRODUCTION

AMERICANA was born in 1932, between the mini-golf boom and the jigsaw puzzle craze. Unlike those phenomenally profitable distractions of the early Depression, the new magazine of pictorial satire did not sweep the country. Nor did it inspire the numerous pages of critical analysis devoted to the Tom Thumb golf and puzzle fads, obvious metaphors for a wounded nation's search for control and wholeness. On the contrary, even the magazine's chief contributors, loquacious in their recall of other episodes from the past, hasten through the *Americana* period in their memoirs and never mention the periodical in their *Who's Who* entries. While the patented hollow-log hazard and other features of the miniature golf course may still be found along any interstate and the jigsaw under any Christmas tree, *Americana* has all but disappeared from the culture for which it was named.

After four irregular issues between February and July, the editor paused to regroup his associates and launched Volume One all over again in November 1932. Twelve monthly issues appeared, and then the first issue of Volume Two forecast a dramatic change of policy to be elucidated in the following number. There was no following number. As if acting out one of its own roughshod jokes, *Americana* vanished forever. Today the only complete set known to have survived is preserved like a Gutenberg Bible under temperature and humidity control in the Rare Books Division at the Library of Congress.

The irony of *Americana*'s ceremonial enshrinement concurrent with a near-total oblivion would have appealed to the persistently Viennese sensibilities of its creator, Alexander King (1899–65). Though he might have relished the image of scholars snickering in the library hush over Al Hirschfeld's Hitler caricatures, King attached little importance to the magazine in his four-volume autobiography. Recalling his subsequent career as a *Life* employee, King could not accurately state the year he had "published a sort of picture magazine of my own."

The year was 1932. Lewis Mumford described it in the December *Atlantic Monthly*:

> The world of 1932 was a sad, drab, harried, disordered place. Millions of people, with no daily work to do, anxiously counted their hours; for our civilization, preoccupied with moving machinery, has lost even its poor peculiar method of filling its emptiness: the wheels did not move.

Novelist Theodore Dreiser put it similarly in the opening sentence of *Tragic America*, published early that same year: "The tempo of this great land is one of speed and contention." Dreiser was known to be gloomy—*Literary Digest* had called him "dark blue Dreiser" two years before—and his book was dismissed by most critics as polemical. But Edmund Wilson praised it in *The New Republic* for giving a significant picture of the present crisis: "the style is always collapsing, but the man behind it remains sound." Wilson in more

WASHINGTON, D. C.

Buddies!

Fig. 1 Victor Candell, *Americana*, November 1932

sprightly prose registered similar reactions during his own trip through the country. The title of his 1932 collection of reportage gave the national mood a better name — *The American Jitters*.

Charting the psychological temperature of the Depression in his 1933 study, *Years of the Locust*, Gilbert Seldes, an associate editor for *Americana*, identified the summer of 1932 as the low point for the country's morale. Since early spring thousands of World War I veterans had gathered in the capital to demand immediate payment of compensation owed them by the Government. In mid-July tear gas exploded on Pennsylvania Avenue when General Douglas MacArthur in command of Federal troops confronted the Bonus Expeditionary Force, as the veterans called themselves, and drove them out of Washington, leveling their encampment of "Hoover villas" in Anacostia Flats. Artist

Victor Candell's drawing for the November *Americana* refers to this event (Fig. 1), as does the piece by poet E. E. Cummings in the same issue (see p. 49). Cummings' President Hooses delivers a Sermon on the Mount, declaring in a new Beatitude: "Blessed are they which are persecuted for bonus' sake, for theirs is the kingdom of tear gas."

That Cummings in this election issue spoofed Roosevelt and Norman Thomas along with Hoover demonstrates the even-handed disgust for party politics enunciated in the policy statement on the editorial page (p. 45). Yet, cynicism in those difficult months was one of the country's least popular *ism*s. The crisis in human culture diagnosed by Wilson in a manifesto written in May (signed by Mumford, John Dos Passos, Waldo Frank, Sherwood Anderson, and others) called for commitment and action. Dreiser at 60 lumbered courageously into Harlan County, Kentucky, to investigate the "lawless terror" corporations were inflicting on coal miners. *Americana* responded with a joke about the State of Kentucky's trumped-up indictment of the aging author on a morals charge for misconduct with a young woman (Fig. 2). As intellectual America shifted soberly leftward, the magazine's doctrinaire endorsement of the horse laugh in the face of futility must have taken a great deal of courage.

Despite its firm disclaimer, the magazine had two living links with the glorious American political art of the past; interestingly, their works appear only in the early issues. John Sloan's soft yet emotionally pointed chalk drawings of working-class life had graced the remarkable magazine *Masses* (1911–17), which he had served as art editor. Sloan apparently gave King several lithographs commissioned and published by *Century* in 1923 to use again in *Americana*. Another veteran of *Masses* was the dean of leftist cartoonists, Art Young. His drawings appeared in each of *Americana*'s first four issues, and his logo depicting Adam and Eve (Fig. 3), first used in November 1932, adorned the masthead page for the life of the magazine. This logo, with its traditional iconography, exposes one difference between *Americana* and its brilliant radical ancestor of two decades earlier. Young's Eve drawn for *Masses*, in line with the publication's strong feminist sympathies, declines the apple. "No thanks," she tells the snake. "There's going to be a lot of trouble, and I don't want to get blamed for it."

After *Masses* was suppressed during World War I, the amiable Young had edited his own satirical magazine, *Good Morning* (1919–21), and drawn for *Liberator* (1918–24), as well as for the bourgeois press. In his mid-sixties and nearly destitute in 1932 when *Americana* began, Young was a contributing editor of *New Masses* (1926–48). Following the tradition of its namesake, this periodical still ran some fine art, but seemed bent on literally embodying the Communist Party policy of "boring from within." Apart from Young, the only other artist publishing in both *New Masses* and *Americana* in 1932–33 was the gifted lithographer from Minnesota, Vienna-trained Adolf Dehn. Dehn had returned from Europe with one magazine credit that would have impressed the *Americana* sophisticates. He had published in *Simplicissimus*.

This audacious illustrated weekly founded in Munich in 1896 was cherished throughout the German-speaking world. Henry Miller recalled that it was on sale at Manhattan newsstands in his youth. Still vigorous in 1932, *Simplicissimus* was relentlessly mocking Hitler in cartoons by Karl Arnold and others. Back issues of *der Simpl*, as the German magazine was called, must have been well thumbed by King as he looked for

"Madam, you flatter me!"

Fig. 2 Alexander King, *Americana*, April 1932

Fig. 3 Art Young, logo for *Americana*, November 1932

The new Cabinet? These faces certainly look familiar.

Fig. 4 Thomas Theodor Heine, *Simplicissimus*, 1928 (No. 14)

(Opposite)
Fig. 5 Covers of American humor magazines from the early 1930s: *Ballyhoo*, February 1932; *Judge*, May and March 1933; and *Life*, October 1931

inspiration; several *Americana* drawings — "The Legitimate and Illegitimate Stork" (p. 173), for example — are updates of earlier cartoons. King also reprinted drawings by Alfred Kubin and Olaf Gulbransson, and selected as an associate former *Simplicissimus* contributor George Grosz. In fact, the strongest influence on King's magazine was the *Simpl* spirit not its style. While widely varying techniques appeared on the pages of *Americana*, most *Simplicissimus* artists worked in pure line or in broad areas of well-defined washes, suitable for the subtle color capabilities of their press. The acerbic *Simpl* captions and the boisterous disrespect of drawings like Thomas Theodor Heine's "The Return of the Same" (Fig. 4), however, match perfectly the prankish exuberance of the best work in *Americana*.

Though it is difficult now to trace the European strain that merged so successfully with other styles in the melting pot of *Americana* art, one astute contemporary critic detected a strong native influence — the patchwork-covered *Ballyhoo* (Fig. 5), a Dell publication launched in 1931. *Ballyhoo* was the *Mad* of its day, with a running joke in the character of Elmer Zilch and his countless family members who signed all the articles. Hilarious parodies of advertising formed the bulk of every issue. In these early years of the Depression when *Vanity Fair* ran ads for luxury automobiles or even airplanes, *Ballyhoo* readers were urged to purchase elegant cars such as the Huffmobile ("Leave in a Huff!"), or Tarzan chest wigs modeled by the *New Yorker*'s emblematic Eustace Dilley. Early issues were wrapped in cellophane ("a fresh magazine"), and one month a demure second cover with the title *The Lilywhite Journal* was provided for readers too timid

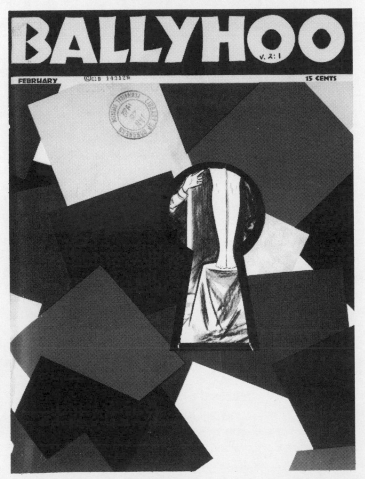

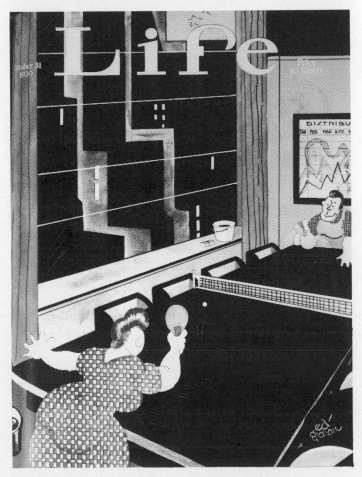

Fig. 6 The Grosz family in Douglaston, Long Island, 1940

to be caught reading such a rowdy publication. *Ballyhoo* was an immediate success, and its editor Norman Anthony, formerly of *Judge* and *Life*, soon was selling real ads and riding around Manhattan in a chauffeur-driven Packard.

Ballyhoo was more or less a one-man operation, and when Anthony's comic genius went flat, the joke seemed very thin indeed. *Americana* too was born of the comic energy of an individual, but, unlike Anthony, Alexander King acted as a magnet for a grand assortment of kindred spirits and attracted during the seventeen-issue run of his magazine an astonishing sample of the best literary and artistic talents of the period. New York first learned of the magazine in the *Times* of January 22, 1932:

NEW ART PICTORIAL TO APPEAR

It is announced that *Americana*, a new monthly pictorial, will make its initial appearance on Monday, under the editorship of Alexander King, with Cleon Throckmorton and Majeska as associate editors. It will be a periodical devoted entirely to drawings, with no text other than the captions. Contributing artists

are Jose Clemente Orozco, William Cotton, Percy Crosby, James Hirsch, Paul Busch, Victor Helleu, Ben Kopman, Miguel Covarrubias, Art Young, Eugene Fitsch, Peggy Bacon and George Grosz.

King had seemingly assembled an all-star cast. His associate Cleon Throckmorton (1897–1965) was among the best-known stage designers in New York; his very first set — for Eugene O'Neill's *Emperor Jones* in 1920 — had made theatrical history. In 1927 he had visited Charleston, South Carolina, before designing the original Catfish Row for the Theatre Guild production of Dorothy and Du Bose Heyward's *Porgy*. Some of the artists for King's first issue were equally famous: Orozco was at the crest of the Mexican mural movement's American phase; his young compatriot Covarrubias was the most popular caricaturist on the stylish *Vanity Fair*, where Cotton published his stunning pastels; Crosby's syndicated strip *Skippy* had just been made into a movie; Eugene Fitsch had designed sets for Cummings' *Him*; Bacon was a leading printmaker; and Grosz, still in Berlin when *Americana* began, was admired for his satirical series of the 1920s, such as *Ecce*

Homo. In spite of this array of names, the magazine attracted no critical attention until King announced on October 4, 1932, that George Grosz had actually joined his staff. Soon after that, on October 19, the following appraisal of the November issue appeared in *The Nation*:

> Equipped with a small staff of artists and writers and one page of advertising, the magazine *Americana* has issued its first regular number. Nor could there be a more appropriate moment for the appearance of this particular publication. It should be studied as a symbol and as a symptom of the times. It is the depression itself wrought in violent black and white. It is bitter without being revolutionary; humorous without being gay; savage and futile. After proclaiming themselves anti-Republican, anti-Democrat, anti-Socialist, and anti-Communist, its editors announce with horrid delight: 'We are Americans who believe that our civilization exudes a miasmic stench and that we had better prepare to give it a decent but rapid burial. We are the laughing morticians of the present.' The morticians in question are Alexander King, Gilbert Seldes, E. E. Cummings, and George Grosz, the German artist. They are assisted by various contributors and, we suspect, by the make-up editor of *Ballyhoo*. This little child of the depression is neither pleasant nor wholesomely, vigorously unpleasant. It is merely unattractively sadistic. We suspect that George Grosz will presently be dropped from the staff. His drawings, to be sure, are sufficiently sardonic, but what of his philosophy? From the very midst of the miasmic stench surrounding him he voices this sentiment: 'I think America is a fine and astonishing land full of virile self-sufficiency. I hope to make my home here.' What kind of a mortician is Mr. Grosz?

The *Nation* article raised a question central to Grosz studies ever since — what of his philosophy? The quote from a brief "Self-Portrait" in the November *Americana* is one of the first records of the immigrant Grosz. His ambition at the time, he later declared in his autobiography, was "to achieve the simplicity and normalcy of American illustration that I so admired…I loved the mediocre, the widely understood language, but to my distress, I was unable quite to master it." His greatest achievement in this direction would be a photograph (Fig. 6) posed in his own Long Island living room some years later. Grosz, with his pipe, was playing chess with one of his sons, while his wife, Eva, sewed under a floor lamp. The result was not a domestic interior by Menzel, a German 19th-century painter Grosz had long admired. Illuminated by Edison and enhanced by Eastman, it was a perfect Rockwell cover.

The covers Grosz meant to draw, to capitalize on, did not come his way. The new Grosz, working with what he later described as a "blurred vision," puzzled critics; "the gladiator is resting," one writer surmised in 1933. Although introduced at once to Harold Ross at the *New Yorker*, Grosz was appreciated and

HOME-LIFE

"Cheer up! If we have four more kids we're liable to get the Roosevelt Propagation Prize."

Fig. 7 George Grosz, *Americana*, July 1932

befriended instead by Alexander King. King, who had run Grosz drawings (Fig. 7) in nearly every issue of *Americana*, gave a welcoming party for him at Muriel Draper's soon after Grosz arrived in New York for the first time on June 3, 1932. His arrival had received avid press coverage because of the controversy at the Art Students League that spring over his appointment to teach in the summer school (John Sloan had resigned in protest when the board balked at inviting Grosz). Interviewed at the dock, Grosz had declared his political independence. His enthusiastic response to his new home was not merely a public stance; his letters to his wife that summer are euphoric, recording in sharp detail the sensations of his initial experience of America. When Grosz sailed back to Germany to fetch her in October — he would return in January 1933, days before Hitler became chancellor — King organized a farewell tea at which he announced to the press that Grosz and Gilbert Seldes would be his co-editors on *Americana*. Grosz reiterated for reporters his interest in the United States, singling out Krazy Kat and Mickey Mouse as distinct contributions to art.

These remarks were appropriate for a new colleague

AMERICAN PASTRIES

The Skyscraper Tart

The New Waldorf Cake

The Sugar-Daddy Tower

The New York Central Cookie

Paramount Pastry

Penthouse Shortcake

Chrysler Layer Cake

Empire State Cream Tart

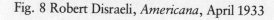

Fig. 8 Robert Disraeli, *Americana*, April 1933

of Gilbert Seldes, who had launched the serious reappraisal of George Herriman's comic strip ten years earlier in *Vanity Fair*. Seldes expanded these views in his pioneering study of 1924, *The Seven Lively Arts*. His book *The Stammering Century* (1928) was equally innovative, examining nineteenth-century American utopian communities. By 1932 Seldes was the country's foremost film critic, and although he was not as wholly bowled over by Mickey Mouse as George Grosz, he declared Disney's *Silly Symphonies* to be movie making at its finest. In the late spring of 1932, shortly before his association with *Americana*, he had angered leftists with his pamphlet *Against Revolution*. It is easy to imagine the appeal of this independent, prolific mind for a brilliant skeptic like Alexander King.

While King might have been able to fill a magazine with the work of his wide circle of gifted friends, his public announcements of editorial staff and policy also attracted newcomers. A young photographer, Robert

Disraeli (like King, the son of German-speaking immigrants to New York) read of the magazine and, after a false trail that led to the American Historical Society's very different publication, tracked King down to his Chelsea apartment, the base of *Americana* operations. Expecting to be ushered into an editorial office with a bustling staff, Disraeli soon realized: "There wasn't any office. There was just Alex and a table and a bottle of India ink. And a telephone. He had to have a telephone." Disraeli describes King at work — dashing off a drawing to fill a blank space or an unsigned cover in his distinctive style of heavy black outlines upon which floats a shading of fine curliques or seismograph lines — ice bag on his head to fight off his chronic migraines. There in the apartment King and his crew dreamed up the wild photo montages that after January 1933 became a distinctive feature of the magazine (Fig. 8). When Disraeli went out on the streets to shoot his pictures, King would sometimes come along to pose.

16

Their collaboration resulted in a unique series of prints, some comical, some deeply moving, a Dada-Depression New York uncharted by Berenice Abbott.

King turned to journalism after *Americana* ran out of money in 1933, until after the war, when an addiction to opium brought about by a prescription pain cure robbed him of a decade of his life. Yet even during stays in a federal narcotics hospital, the ebullient King edited and illustrated magazines. Cured at last, he published *Mine Enemy Grows Older* in 1958. This was the first of four volumes of memoirs, all best sellers — not only because of their rich literary merits, but because Alexander King (Fig. 9) had invented yet another means of expression as a television personality. A routine guest appearance on the Jack Paar show marked the beginning of a provocative assault on the institutionalized prudery and pervasive somnolence that had turned television — meant to be one of Gilbert Seldes's lively arts — into the dreary headless beast now known as the mass media. King's last book, *Rich Man, Poor Man, Freud and Fruit* came out on his sixty-sixth birthday in 1965, and he appeared on television to promote it on the morning of his death a few days later.

Americana friends were loyal to the end. S. J. Perelman and Al Hirschfeld had persuaded their own publisher to look at the manuscript of King's first book, and the second volume of memoirs was dedicated to Al, Dolly, and Nina Hirschfeld. King's widow recalls the enormous solace offered her by the widow of E. E. Cummings, who had died three years earlier. Apart from friendship with King, the *Americana* contributors share a remarkable combination of literary and artistic talents. Few samples of artists turn up so many with published prose in various fields. King, Grosz, Hirschfeld, Lynd Ward, and Young have all written autobiographies; King, Peggy Bacon, Howard Baer, Disraeli, William Steig, and Ward, distinguished children's books; King and Cotton, plays; Bacon and Seldes, thrillers; and Covarrubias, anthropology. Of the *Americana* writers, E. E. Cummings and Nathanael West both started out as painters, and S. J. Perelman drew for *Judge* before becoming known as a satirist. This unique conjunction of gifts, marshalled briefly in the service of laughter, remains unsurpassed in recent American literary history.

Fig. 9 Alexander King, early 1960s, photographed by Hans Namuth

*For this anthology Robert Disraeli, who has recently returned to still photography after a long career in film-making, has reprinted some of his *Americana* work from fifty-year-old negatives.

THE GREAT DEPRESSION

AMERICANA *"should be studied as a symbol and as a symptom of the times. It is the depression itself wrought in violent black and white."*

The Nation *(Oct. 19, 1932)*

"Prosperity is Just Around the Corner."
HERBERT HOOVER

DEPRESSION

SHORT HISTORY OF A DEPRESSION

by GILBERT SELDES

(The dates given below are corrected to only three decimal places. The information is all derived from speakeasy conversations of retired customer's men.)

OCTOBER 1, 1929: It could not occur.

OCTOBER 23, 1929: It wasn't occurring.

NOVEMBER 1, 1929: It hadn't happened.

NOVEMBER 15, 1929: It was purely a technical operation in the market.

NOVEMBER 20, 1929: It had restored brains to thinking and money to productive enterprise.

NOVEMBER 27, 1929: Thanksgiving.

DECEMBER 12, 1929: It was the result of overproduction and consequently men must not be fired, wages must not be lowered, so that production should not be cut down.

DECEMBER 13, 1929: It was the result of underconsumption, so the victims (the guilty ones) must spend freely, instantly, to take up the slack.

DECEMBER 20, 1929: Huge bonuses voted to chairmen of boards *pour encourager les autres*.

DECEMBER 25, 1929: Merry Christmas.

JANUARY 5, 1930: Corporations report vastly increased earnings. Starving man dies of measles in a charity ward.

JANUARY 15, 1930: Irving Fisher predicts a crash sometime in next two years if we are not careful.

FEBRUARY 7, 1930: "The corner" takes the place in American mythology once held by "the West."

MARCH 1-17, 1930: Calvin Coolidge calculates that prosperity will return; mathematically trained Hoover makes calculation finer and gives date of rendezvous.

MARCH 20, 1930: Good News of Good Times. Also Buy Now. Workingmen, unable to understand plain English, riot for jobs.

APRIL 6, 1930: It was all the fault of Europe. Congress continues to play with the tariff.

APRIL 20, 1930: Purely psychological.

MAY 3, 1930: Discovered that Calvin Coolidge sold his U. S. Steel shares before October 23, 1929. No Congressional investigation is ordered.

MAY 17, 1930: Prosperity fails to keep date with President Hoover. Reported eaten by bears.

MAY 25, 1930: Motor car manufacturers decide to restore prosperity by selling motor cars to each other.

JUNE 3, 1930: Inasmuch as nothing was lost (except paper profits) the condition of America is sound. The sound is hollow.

JULY 9, 1930: Not one person has frozen to death in the past three months in continental America. Virgin Islands and Hawaii not yet heard from.

AUGUST 16, 1930: Satisfaction expressed in knowledge that this is the greatest depression in history and we are suffering more than any one else.

SEPTEMBER—DECEMBER 3, 1930: Intellectuals give it all up and go Communist. Communists inhospitable to intellectuals, engage American engineers to industrialize Russia.

JANUARY 3, 1931: U. S. enters happy new year in the red, to spite Hoover, and the greatest secretary of the treasury since Ponzi.

JANUARY—FEBRUARY 4, 1931: Theory of cycles brings great happiness to all. Dullwits ask what's the use of cycles without starters. Pres. Hoover repeats his wish that wages should not go down; Newton's experiment with apple recalled.

FEBRUARY 9, 1931: It's smart to be thrifty engraved on U. S. coins (displacing well-known but uneconomic theory of trusting in God.) Coins go into hoarding.

MAY 2, 1931: Reader of Herald-Tribune suggests that if all luck pieces were banked, prosperity would return. No action is taken.

MAY 2, 1931: Red Cross proves God superior to Man by providing for victims of drought and flood, but not of strikes. Rugged individualism begins to be considered a typographical error.

JUNE—JULY 4, 1931: Flushed with prosperity, U. S. remits foreign debts for a year. Protests of France causes great distrust of foreigners in Washington. Mr. Hoover's voice fails to carry on Trans-Atlantic telephone; M. Laval's voice does not.

JULY 19, 1931: Charles K. Curtis, a vice-president, emerges from obscurity to say better times are coming. Obscurity instantly restored.

SEPTEMBER 2, 1931: Wages defy wishes of Administration and go down. Solution of depression found in economy, balanced budgets, and huge building program to employ two thousand men alternate Tuesdays and Thursdays, preferably without pay.

SEPTEMBER 9, 1931: Nerve-wracking suspicion enters American mind that Henry Ford is not infallible.

OCTOBER 12, 1931: Beer suggested as ladder industry. Amos 'n' Andy wane. Radio hours now quarter hours, multiplying advertising time by sixteen (mathematical progression).

NOVEMBER 15, 1931: President's Thanksgiving Proclamation makes nineteenth page of paper published in England, Arkansas.

NOVEMBER 22, 1931: Depression enters final stage. Twins in Oklahoma named Norman and Thomas.

DECEMBER 31, 1931: In accordance with orders issued at various points, the depression ends.

MAY 29, 1932: Stocks hit lowest level, unemployment hit highest level, Dawes takes control of Reconstruction Finance Corporation, Dawes leaves Reconstruction Finance Corporation, Dawes banks borrow 80,000,000 dollars from Reconstruction Finance Corporation, and an American army, by executive order, fires on American citizens, signalizing the return of prosperity and the beginning of a presidential campaign.

WINTER 1932

"THEY ALSO SERVE WHO ONLY STAND AND WAIT"

THE SIDEWALKS OF NEW YORK

EAT AT CHARLIE'S — TRY OUR COLONIAL HOME COOKED DINNER 50¢

Mlle. Cohene Salon de Beauté — Let us make your skin ravishing — Facials 50¢

"They're giving me my meals for this. What're you gettin'?"

"I think the depression is behind us."

—"But you too have something to be thankful for, haven't you, my good man?"

—"Yes lady, I'm glad that bed-bugs don't cough."

25

"If this keeps up my tape-worm's gonna starve to death."

"To think that this was once the most promising can in town."

ON TUESDAY LAST—MR. AND MRS. DE PEYSTER HINES OFFICIALLY
TOOK NOTE OF WHAT IS RUMORED TO BE A DEPRESSION.

SOCIETY

"My dear, America is beginning to smell dreadfully of poor people."

Charity: "Our committee found the five-cent meals satisfactory in every way!"

NOTES ON A LOST ART
By IRVING KOLODIN

While it is true that a large number of Americans have found it possible to exist without automobiles, and a pair of even thread-bare gloves is an indication of affluence, no one has yet discovered a plan of subsistence that eliminates eating, although it is true, many have tried. Increasing quantities of our solid burgher-folk have found it convenient to dine out, and to aid their pursuit of epicurean delights, *Americana* has undertaken an extensive survey of the permanently available eateries, that the man of substance . . . say one who has fifty cents in his pocket . . . may avail himself of the best the land affords.

We will begin by dismissing immediately from consideration such abortive places as the numerous Lunch Bars, Milk Bars, Coffee Bars, Doughnut Bars, etc., where one is granted, for a price, the equivalent of sitting in a kitchen while the food is prepared before his eyes, under his very nose. Huddled against a counter, hat on lap, with the leavings of his neighbor's melted cheese sandwich still perfuming the air, he is tortured by the fear of spattering Crisco, momentarily in danger of having his life snuffed out under the mountain of doughnuts tottering in front of him. No, these places are little above the soda-fountains patronized by the wastrels of our society.

There remains, then, that vast, sprawling category, generically known as cafeterias. Prominent among them, through continued excellence and a solid tradition, are those of Messrs. Horn and Hardart, Foltis-Fisher, Bickford, John R. Thompson, and the homely Silver's. Yet even among these generally admirable institutions, a hierarchy exists.

The depots of Messrs. Foltis-Fisher are famed for their baked Idaho (not Long Island, let us insist) potatoes, the tasty goodness tumbling out of their bursting jackets, while their Roast Philadelphia capon is a poem. But they, too, have a fetish, a crusading attitude toward the Vegetable Kingdom, which they urge upon one at every turn. Why a man with a craving for an inspiriting platter of *Tripes a la mode de Caen* should have a mess of depressing cauliflower, drowned spinach and pulverized squash forced upon him, I can't quite see. And huge stacks of whole-wheat bread intimidate the patron who wants merely wheat bread. It is produced if one insists, but it is too much trouble, and hardly worth while. Towards Silver's, we have a curiously apathetic attitude. Their salads are the product of something bordering on genius, and they display a regal disdain for commercialism every now and then with "Free Soup Days", when a foaming *potage* is dispensed, on the house, with each *plate de jour.* Yet we have noticed that it is a favorite resort of the young men about town, who pollute the generally sedate air with loud remarks about the turf, games of chance and "wrassling," disturbing the concentration of those intent upon literature and the arts.

Which brings us, naturally, to the superior establishments of John R. ("Daddy") Thompson, where thirty-five cents is wealth and fifty cents is super-

"The food isn't very good here but the place is cozy."

fluous riches. Candor compels the observation that certain locations have influenced the character of even these fine hospices, but the finest flower of the Thompson dynasty is to be found at 1130 Sixth Avenue opposite a huge desolate-looking structure still referred to as the Hippodrome.

Coat trees are provided to flatter your two-winter-old Chesterfield, and an air of quiet dignity pervades the whole. We indicate no choice of dishes, for the whole of their ample *menu* is beyond criticism. For the inexperienced we suggest a small steak a la Thompson, garnished with crisply tanned potatoes and garden peas, which, plus dessert and coffee is a mere forty cents. Over your second cup of coffee, with the scent of a Superba Deliciosa Charles Denby Perfecto (at five cents) in your nostrils, the world passes in review via the columns of the New York Mail-Globe-World-Telegram and Commercial Advertiser. At a near-by table, a dilettante is completing "War and Peace" started at breakfast the day before . . . a student checks the references of Gibbon's "Decline and Fall" . . . a young composer puts the finishing touches on a re-orchestration of "Elektra". Here the gastronome finds joy; the sybarite ease and luxury; the intellectual, an atmosphere congenial to his inner harmonies, truly an American counterpart of the Viennese Coffeehouse.

I defer to the excellence of the Spanish Rice at these colloquially known as the Automat, and their New York Coffee-cake (retailing at a nickel) is, in truth, a delicacy. But when the unpleasant business of stuffing one's self has been concluded, to equip one again for the civilized functions of smoking, conversation or reading the editorial page of the *Evening Post* what happens? An attendant dressed like a hospital orderly marches up and announces, "You can't smoke here." Is this the answer to Valley Forge? Is this the reward for the blood-stained soil of Gettysburg? Are we, or are we not, Free? And, too, they are full of Tourists Having their Fling . . . converting crisp dollar-bills from the hinterlands into nickels . . . coffee flowing like water . . . investing two nickels in Boston coffee-cake when the New York article is equally good, for only one. This vulgar display of wealth is repulsive to any sober-minded citizen.

Much the same objection may be cited against the otherwise satisfactory Bickford's. Their *Oeufs poeles au Jambon* are subtly, but unmistakeably, the archtype of their kind, redolent and just sufficiently browned. Their Boston Brown Bread and Baked Beans is a treasured secret among gourmets. But here, too, a misguided censorship is in force. They shake a moral finger at tobacco, while seeking to encourage the use of it elsewhere by a greedy traffic on the contraband at the door as one exits. This hair-splitting deserves no encouragement from the judicious.

"I'm not hungry for food—I'm hungry for love!"

FROM SOUP TO NUTS

By BOB BROWN

The 1933 mail order catalogues are out; replete with sartorial suggestions for the complete outfitting of both the well-dressed male and his female *élégante*.

From the exhaustive lists given of human requisites both chic and everyday, two representative Americanos have been painstakingly assembled in every detail, at a price within reach of all:

THE FORGOTTEN MAN
Complete for $39.99

Pilgrim Athlete Under-shirt, Swiss Ribbed. Soft, easy-fitting Pull over	$ .19
Shorts. 3-button yoke front Double panel, skillfully shaped, deep circular seat. Reinforced crotch	.49
Police and Firemen's Quality Suspenders. Genuine Cow-hide ends, full 40 in. long, 22 added inches of stretch. Double-stitched Comfort Pad in Back. Metal Hook Supports Trouser Weight. Brass Fittings	.69
Garter, Necktie, Belt and Arm-band Set. All of the same jaunty colored ribbon. Single Grip Paris Green Web Garters. Elastic Arm-bands. Teck Tie, tied into permanent four-in-hand. Hard to detect difference. Genuine Harness Bull Leather Belt decorated with Nickel Plated Rounded Studs. Riveted in. Plenty of "punch" and endurance	2.49
Uncle Sam Socks. Good substantial Cotton, elastic ribbed tops. Weight 2 lbs. the dozen pair	.09
The Shoe Price News of 1933! Full 16 in. high dark brown "Eskimo" oil tanned split cow-hide leather uppers. Full leather midsole, 13-nail Rubber Heel. Sizes up to 12. Wide Widths only	2.49
Shirt, choice of navy blue or khaki, medium weight flannel of about ⅓ wool, balance cotton. Deep double Yoke in Back. Ventilating eyelets under arm-pits. Triple stitched seams and unbreakable buttons	1.49
Dependable Ice Men's Tough Pants. Brutes for Wear! They're made of Kersey. Pockets are of boat sail drill and will last as long and Give as Good Service as the Pants. Oxford Gray Striped	2.99
The Judge Style Cap. A Prime Favorite for wearing year in and year out, inside and out. It is so warm, so stoutly made of All Wool Thibet Cloth. Indestructible Canvas Visor	.79
The Popular Patch Palm Reversible Mittens, with the nap on the outside. Made of A.1 Canton Flannel with *Two Thumbs* for Double Wear	.09
His Jewelry is Impeccable. Since scarf pins are "in" again, he wears a 10-karat solid white gold article of genuine black onyx with rose-cut diamond gleaming in the center, $3.49; his front collar button is of real gold, .89; the unpretentious back collar button, greenish gold filled effect costs .09. His Ring is Manly. Genuine Black Onyx with Red Gold trim and one initial (Print initial plainly), $4.99. He carries a New Signet Watch Outfit with Blue Enameled Initial and raised gilt numerals, $3.76. Total for jewelry	13.22
In his roomy pockets he carries: (a) Pocket Tin of Breethem, the Popular Breath Deodorant, 9c; (b) Stuart's Dyspepsia Tablets, 49c; (c) Handy Tin of Cascarets, 9c; (d) Box of Allen's Foot Ease, 29c; (e) ½ Lb. Bag Horehound Candy, 9c; (f) A snap-shot of her, 9c. Total pocket equipment	1.14
Swinging over his manly shoulder is an Assortment of Oneida Victor Traps, good for Muskrats, Mink, Oppossums and Skunks. 4-in. Jaw Spread. Three for	.59
He carries assorted bottles of Burbank's Improved Animal Scents:	
1. Mink Scent	.69
2. Coon Scent	.49
3. Muskrat	.59
4. Fox	.69
5. Skunk & Possum Scent	.49
6. Trail Scent, to Lure the animal into the trap	.59
He wears a bandana handkerchief, the extra large 27 in. size, nonchalantly knotted about his Adam's Apple. Red or Blue	.09
He never goes anywhere without One indexed Memo Book, full of telephone numbers	.49
And hip flask of Genuine Bay Rum, useful to repel mosquitoes and relieve headaches	.69

He is 100% He-Man.
A Man's Man, and a
Woman's too, for a' That

THE ABANDONED WOMAN
Outfitted Entire, Only $39.99

Vest, Princess Style, Lustrous finish like Satin. Reinforced under arms	$ .79
De Luxe Lingerie, roomy, well-made panties, with double gusset crotch and extra 76 in. seat	.89
"Form Bust for New Style Curves." Has cleverly shaped invisible bust pads, removable, soft and fluffy, imparting the appearance of the Grace and Beauty of a Natural Bust	.69
Tu-Way Stretch Foundation Lastex Back and Sides. Smart Peach-Blush Shade. *You'll feel Free in this.* Makes you wonderfully flexible. Controls and restrains in just the right quarters. Semi-Step-in Style. Has hooks at side to hip line. Diaphragm control. Well-boned back. Adjustable inner belt and Liberal elastics	2.99
Carefree stockings, Nude. They stretch to fit the Larger Leg	.79
Good-looking Shoes. Fine Reptile Effect Trim. Built-in Steel Arch Support. Two inch covered spike heels for ankle slimness. Specially designed to reduce strain on Fleshy Feet	2.49
There's Many a Slip. . . . But we recommend the Princess Pat Slip, because of its "V" style bodice, its nice, high class finish, its stylish shape, with full flare Bottom	.79
"Everyone's Darling" Dress. With every flutter of the cape collar, a bright red lining flashes out. Red flower and sash gaily repeat tone. Slinky bias-cut Skirt fits all figures	3.99
The Impressor Hat. We're just Wild about this Tricky Little Number with its Debonair Chic Grosgrain Ribbon Cockade and its general Negligent, Go-to-Blazes Air	1.79
Cotton Chamoisuede fabric Gloves. Narrow piping in Contrasting Color gives Cuffs that Modish Tier Effect. Hairline Stitched Back, Knip-Knot Fingers and Balloon Thumbs	.69
Her Jewelry is Irresistible. A simple but elegant brooch in solid silver, with the correct stone and flower of her birth-month. (Be sure to state Month,) 89c; Ear-screws asparkle with imitation Diamonds, 59c; Festoon Necklace, green Gold color, attractive leaf design with Pearl Drops, 79c. Her ring is Exquisitely Feminine; set with White synthetic Sapphire and easily mistaken for Engagement Ring, $3.49. Total for Jewelry	5.76
In her smart Two-Way Handle Man-Trap Bag she carries: (a) Hand-hammered effect Lighter, $1.99; (b) Sterling Silver effect Black Cocoa Bead Rosary, 29c; (c) Silveroid Thimble, 19c; (d) Cutex Set, 49c; (e) Supply of "Hush" and "Mum" and small phial of "Muscle Oil" for use around the eyes, (estimated) 9c; (f) Four snap-shots of Him, 29c. Total pocket-book equipment	3.34
Swinging in her dainty hand is The Senorita Compact, newest Loose powder container, rouge and lip stick Incarnate, 2 puffs. Choice of three colors for	.99
She carries assorted purse-size phials of scent, too:	
1. Breath of Spring	.49
2. Lily of the Valley	.39
3. Sweet Pea	.19
4. Jasmine	.59
5. *Deja le Printemps*	.89
6. Trailing Arbutus	.59
She never goes out without 2 aspirin tablets, tissue wipers, tube of vaseline and fever thermometer. (Estimated)	1.04
Her engagements and notes she keeps in the "Dear Diary" date book, with addresses in back	.39
A friend has presented her with a purse flask containing one gill of genuine gin	.00

She is irresistibly feminine and always in demand wherever men gather.

Both go to bed in Our Lowest Priced Nifty Night Wear, 3% Pure Wool and half a Yard Wide.

Gents'	.49	Ladies'	.49

Let us look in upon them as they disrobe, if it does not seem too indelicate a thing to do.

They remove, before retiring, the following essentials, in the order given:

French Style Spring Truss, Lightweight, comfortable	2.79	Elastic Front, a good quality reducing supporter	2.09
Army and Navy Style Suspensory. The Most Popular	.39	Jubilee Dress Shields. Flesh Colors Only	.29
Spiral Spring Arch Support. Excellent for Weak Feet	2.99	Seamless Garter Stocking. Relieves Swollen Limbs	2.99
Neat Leather Bunion Protector	.59	3 Blue Jay Corn Plasters	.09
Toe Spreader—Keeps Crooked Toes Straight	.19	Metatarsal Support, Relieves Metatarsalgia or Morton's Toe	2.89
Flesh Color Guaranteed Elastic Stocking	.99	Silk Woven Knee Cap. Swell for Swollen Knees	.59
TOTALS	**$39.99**		**$39.99**

FASHIONS
FORECAST FOR 1932

A return to the bare necessities.

ADVANCE SPRING STYLES

Schiaparelli Sport Coat observed on
Park Ave. and 111th Street

Informal Afternoon Dress by Molineux
(note the new high waistline.)
Fifth Avenue and 125th Street

A Walking Outfit by Patou
serviceable and elegant
Broadway and 212th Street

A distingue ensemble for the working girl
by Chanel
Riverside Drive and 114th Street

The artist printed this drypoint in 1932 using the title Allure.

PEGGY BACON

"Every woman can, and should, cultivate that tantalizing something."
— FANNIE HURST

SALVATION

"And only six months ago I was a bum!"

A STORY-TELLER'S HOLIDAY

By MURIEL DRAPER

He arrives in the late afternoon.

He is quiet, decent, and proudly sad.

The stamp of experience upon him is so immediately impressive that the passage of years over his person is difficult to trace: he could be almost thirty, almost forty, almost fifty years of age.

He is short, compact, and a Negro, with eyes that are fountains of innocence, honesty, and grief.

He comes into your presence as if it were the one right he was still free to enjoy in an otherwise alien world. His manner suggests that he and his God are resigned to wrong-doing and injustice. He manages to convey, somewhat doubtfully, a hope that you too may understand. He introduces himself by telling you frankly that he has been sent to you by a friend who wishes to help him, but being unable to do so for one reason or another—always a good one—has trustfully delegated the kindly duty to you. He then names the friend, who proves to be some person whom you know, or is known in the world formed by your tastes, sympathies, and activities. The type of person he selects varies according to the type of listener. In my experience of him, he has named artists, explorers, philosophers, educators and radicals. In choosing an individual from this wide and fanciful array, three features remain the same. The person is of independent character, notable accomplishment, and absent from New York.

His information is correct, extensive and intimate; his conjectures are logical and tolerant. On this firm basis he builds up a most skillfully flattering appeal to your serious attention. Into this he weaves the thread of a story—*his* story—which he picks up, drops, picks up again, with just the right degree of tantalizing hesitation. Not until he has aroused you to unquestioning interest does he start his narrative, beginning with the dramatic inquiry:

"What do you think of criminals?"

With immense satisfaction at being given the chance to express the protective mercifulness of your thoughts about criminals, you tell him. A look of delight at not having misjudged you passes over his countenance, and he proceeds to the next question.

"Have you ever been in jail?"

Dejectedly you confess that you have not. (Some may answer arrogantly in the affirmative.) These two questions quivering in the air, he leaps forth into the main stream of his story, which is, with varying details, as follows:

He arrived in New York five years ago, in search of knowledge, improvement, and work. At the end of ten days, he was given the promise of a job in Harlem, and, jumping into a car opportunely offered by a casual friend, started uptown to secure it. In his excitement he overlooked the fact that he had no license. Going faster and faster in eager pursuit of work, he rushed through the park and out into 110th Street just in time to knock down a faltering old man, who was at the moment attempting to cross the street. He stopped the car to pick the poor creature up, but alas, too late. A yellow taxi-cab, speeding down 110th Street, passed over the old man and killed him.

You can imagine his fate. Without close friends in New York, only the promise of a job, a battered car he did not own, no automobile licence, a dead old man, his word against a corporation lawyer's . . . The outcome was predictable, if unfortunate. He was convicted of homicide, and sent to jail for ten years.

He is just out on parole, due to behaviour modestly described as normal, but reluctantly revealed in fact as Spartan. He proceeds to outline his plans for the future. An old friend who, with God and himself and happily included you, *understands*, also leads an orchestra in a Los Angeles hotel; in true Christian spirit, this friend has offered him a position as a pianist in his orchestra. By the terms of his parole, he must be employed within a certain number of days from the date of his dismissal. If he leaves New York that night, he will be dutifully at work in time. Otherwise. . . .

The story in this condensed form may sound crude and incredible. You should hear him tell it! It takes him from one to three hours, and it is supported by a psychological cunning not to be conveyed by the printed word.

He does not have to *ask* you for help. You ask *him* how he is going to get to Los Angeles. He tells you that he has saved the money earned in jail, and that a little more will get him there by bus. He does not know exactly how much will be needed, but he tries to figure it out. You do not wait for him to compute it. You give him all you have. You telephone to sympathetic friends who give more. You send telegrams to other friends in California, asking them to look out for him upon arrival. You put flowers in his buttonhole. You thank him for coming to you. You linger over his amazing story. You are ashamed of any fleeting doubts you may have entertained of its verity.

You do *not* ask him to play the piano. You do *not* ask to see his dismissal papers. You do *not* ask for proof of the offer of a job. In fact, you do not do anything but give, because you are so grateful to know one courageous soul who, in spite of injustice, hardship and disappointment, survives the trials of a wicked world without complaint. You bid him Godspeed, and he departs for Los Angeles, his pockets full of money.

On a small scale, he is the most successful psychological manipulator I have ever encountered. He has made more people glad to give money than any single individual I know. Indeed, I wonder if anyone has ever refused him.

If he could be persuaded to forego the extreme pleasure he must extract from the present exercise of his shameless powers, he could be of great service in high places.

Statue of Lincoln by Gutzon Borglum (sculptor of Mt. Rushmore),

installed in 1911 at the Essex Co. Courthouse, Newark, New Jersey

AMERICAN FAIRY-TALES

THE SIDEWALKS OF NEW YORK

"Shoelaces?"

THE ARMY BUILDS MEN!

UNEMPLOYED VETERAN

HEROES OF PEACE

THE ELECTION
AND A NEW DEAL

NEW YORK GOVERNOR Franklin Delano Roosevelt (1882–1945) was nominated on the fourth ballot at the Democratic convention in June 1932. On November 8, he defeated the Republican incumbent Herbert Hoover (1874–1964) by 472 electoral votes to 59. The new president took office only on March 4, 1933, and during this long interregnum no serious measures alleviated the deepening economic crisis. By election day unemployment had passed 13 million, yet most legislative energy at the end of that year was directed toward the repeal of Prohibition. The Great Engineer, as Herbert Hoover was called, pinned his hopes on international solutions to be invented at the World Economic Conference scheduled for 1933. Roosevelt, skeptical of the conference, was planning the series of vigorous monetary, fiscal, and industrial reforms combined with relief programs known as the New Deal.

• EDITORIAL •

We are not REPUBLICANS *because* . . .

the present office holders have dismally failed in leader-
ship and intelligence and because the moneyed oligarchy
that runs and ruins this country is animated by stupid and
shameless greed best exemplified by the Republican party.
As for Mr. Hoover personally, we rest content by presenting the record of his flabbiness and incompetence.

We are not DEMOCRATS *because* . . .

the Democratic party is no less corrupt than the party in
power and is simply striving to glut its vicious and insati-
able appetite at the public money trough. As for Mr.
Roosevelt personally, we consider him a weak and vacil-
lating politician who will be an apt tool in the hands of
his powerful backers.

We are not SOCIALISTS *because* . . .

the erstwhile sentimental liberalism of the Socialists has
degenerated to the bourgeois mouthings of their spokesman, Mr. Norman Thomas.

We are not COMMUNISTS *because* . . .

the American Communist party delegates its emissaries
to bite the rear ends of policemen's horses and finds its
chief glory in spitting at the doormen of foreign legations.
We are also unconditionally opposed to Comrade Stalin
and his feudal bureaucracy at Moscow.

We are Americans who believe that our civilization exudes a
miasmic stench and that we had better prepare to give it a
decent but rapid burial.

We are the laughing morticians of the present.

Editor—ALEXANDER KING   *Associates*—George Grosz, Gilbert Seldes

CAPONE
FOR
PRESIDENT

**The Friend of the Wets
and the Drys**

VIVA CAPONE

The unwarranted persecution of gangsters in this country must cease! These buccaneers and freebooters of the machine age represent the only glamorous and romantic group of men left to us now that the banker and broker have joined the heroes of mythology.

Al Capone, or "Snorky" as he is affectionately called by his hench-men, is the victim of a miscarriage of justice. The government demanded its cut on his racket although it had consistently thwarted him in the full development of his career. He languishes in a federal prison while thousands of widows and orphans whose benign benefactor he had always been, say nightly prayers for the well-being of his person.

"Snorky" distributed alms with a lavish hand, arranged elaborate funerals for his murdered lieutenants, placed their helpless dependents on his payroll and gave employment to thousands of otherwise

unemployable social outcasts. He purchased motor-cars, speedboats, country estates, and by means of telegrams, newsprint, police uniforms, floral wreaths and ammunition, caused millions of dollars to be put in circulation.

He was a facile target for public indignation which must now vent itself on high government functionaries. The inevitable "Constant Reader" has been reduced to writing to his local newspaper about birdlife in the suburbs and the decay of modern youth.

It would be far wiser for us to recall him from his intramural vacation and ask him to assist in the management of our political affairs. It would certainly be preferable to centralize our system of graft and bribery under one head instead of pursuing the ruinous individualistic tactics which obtain at the present time.

"Snorky" can be bought, but at least he would stay bought,—as good a definition of an honest man as we have ever encountered.

FASHIONS
FORECAST FOR 1932

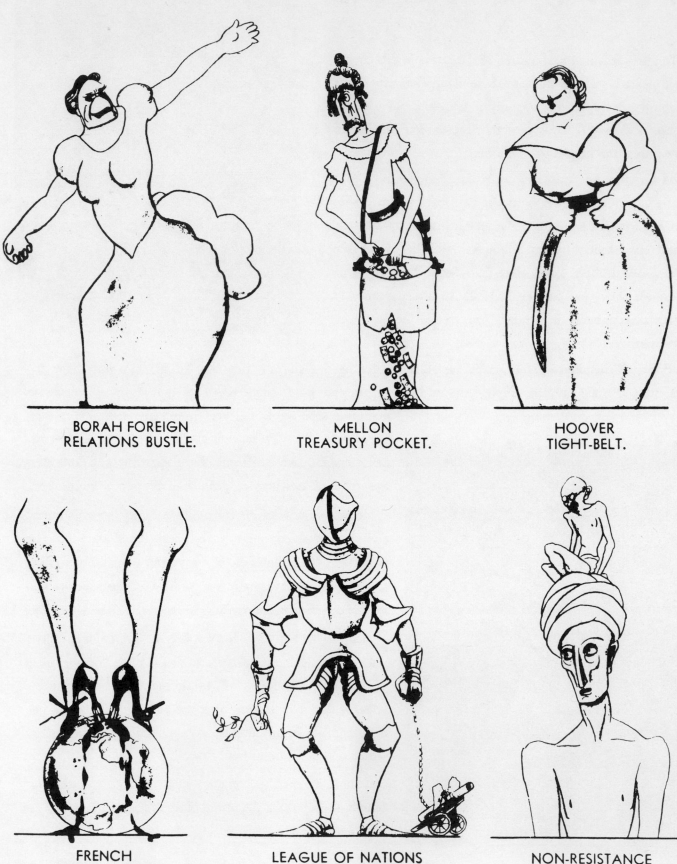

BORAH FOREIGN
RELATIONS BUSTLE.

MELLON
TREASURY POCKET.

HOOVER
TIGHT-BELT.

FRENCH
SPIKED HEELS.

LEAGUE OF NATIONS
SPORT COSTUME

NON-RESISTANCE
TURBAN.

AND IT CAME TO PASS

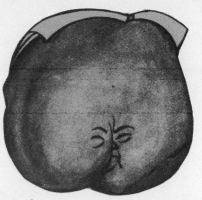

•

by E. E. CUMMINGS

•

(*Scenes an eclipse. Enter President HOOSES, disguised as a wolf in sheep's clothing, walking on water. Everything immediately gets very dark*)

HOOSES (*sheepishly*): Suffer the microphone to come unto me. (*A mike is suffered*). —Be of good cheer; it is I. (*Laughter*). Woe unto you that laugh now! for you shall mourn and weep. (*Mourning and weeping*). Why are ye fearful, O ye of little faith? Why reason ye, because ye have no bread? Man shall not live by bread alone. (*Enter, disguised as himself,* NORMAN THOMAS, *asleep, wearing a halo.*) Get thee behind me, socialism. Are there not twelve hours in the day? He that hath cheeks to turn, let him turn. (*Enter Governor* BOOSEVELT, *disguised as a sheep in wolf's clothing, swimming in beer*).

BOOSEVELT (*wolfishly*): I am the light of the world.

A VOICE: Let's go!

HOOSES: Blessed are the poor in spirit, for they shall inherit the pot of gold at the end of every rainbow. Blessed are they that agitate, for they shall be clubbed. Blessed are the prosperous, for they shall be around the corner. Blessed are they which do hunger and thirst, for they shall obtain unemployment. Blessed are the meek, for they shall be filled with hooey. Blessed are the bull and bear, for they shall lie down together. Blessed are the pieceworkers, for they shall be torn piecemeal. Blessed are they which are persecuted for bonus' sake, for

theirs is the kingdom of tear gas.

A VOICE: We want Waters!

HOOSES: Love thine enemas. Bless them that goose you. (*Offering a bayonet*): Take, eat, this is my body.

NORMAN THOMAS (*asleep*): B-r-r-r . . .

HOOSES: And now to facts. — The trouble with trouble is, that trouble is troublesome. If trouble were not troublesome, we should not have troublous times. If we should not have troublous times, we did not need to worry. If we did not need to worry, our pockets were not so full.

THE GHOST OF GEORGE ABRAHAM: Full of what?

THE VOICE OF AL CAPONE: Neither do men put new wine in old bottles.

HOOSES: Full of hands. Our reconstruction program, involving as it does the unascertainable principle that a depression is the indirect result of direct economic causes, cannot but succeed in seriously mitigating a situation which would otherwise prove ambidextrous to every left-handed right-thinking moron. I therefore sacredly assert, on the one hand, that the time is now ripe for this great nation to evade an issue; and, on the other hand, as an immediate and an eventual solution of this vast country's difficulties, I timidly and confidently propose to fill hands with work by emptying pockets of hands.

A VOICE: Burp.

BOOSEVELT (*taking the mike*): We hold these truths to be self-evident; that all men are created people, and all people are created feeble, and all feeble are created minded, and all minded are created equal.

And the sequal to equal being opportunity, it is obvious that opportunity knocks but once and then it boosts. Nothing can really be done unless you and me are willing to fearlessly confront one another with each other; believing, with the common man, that as long as people are men America is the land of opportunity. (*Three Bronx cheers by a common man named Smith*).

THE GHOST OF JEFFERSON THOMAS: One card.

HOOSES (*taking the mike*): Verily, verily, I say unto you: the kingdom of Wall Street is like to a bottle of iodine, which a man took.

SOMEBODY (*sotto voice*): Thank god we had Bell-Ans!

HOOSES: Cast ye the unprofitable servant into outer darkness. For unto everyone that hath shall be given, and he shall have abundance; but from him that hath not shall be taken away even that which he hath. The foxes have nests and the birds have holes. By their fruits we shall know them. What therefore I have put together let no man join asunder. For there is nothing hid which shall not be manifested; neither was anything kept secret, but that it should come from abroad.

A VOICE: Kruger & Toll.

THE GHOST OF WASHINGTON LINCOLN: I pass.

BOOSEVELT (*seizing the mike, shouts*): Ladies and gentlemen of the invisible audience—follow me and I will make you stinking drunk! (*Piously*): Andrew Jackson who art in heaven, I take this country to be wringing wet. My party will, abolish the still, on election as it was in convention. Take us away our income tax, and forgive us our Judge Seaburys as we do not forgive our Mayor Walkers. And lead us right into the White House, and deliver to us boodle; do not even the republicans the same?

SOMEBODY: So what.

NORMAN THOMAS (*drowsily*): Verily, verily, verily, verily, verily, I say unto you: throw your vote away and follow me.

THE VOICE OF RUDY VALLE: But you want lovin', and I want love.

HOOSES (*taking the mike*): O faithless and perverse generation, the harvest truly is plenteous, but the labourers are few. (*To the ladies*): Take heed that no man deceive you, for many shall come in my name. (*To the children*): Of such is the kingdom of Wall Street. (*To the men*): Except foolish virgins become as a camel entering a needle's eye, ye positively shall not have a chicken in every garage. (*A cock crows*). Amen. (*Thunder and lightning*).

A VOICE (*hysterical*): Pigs is risen!

"BRING 'EM BACK ALIVE"

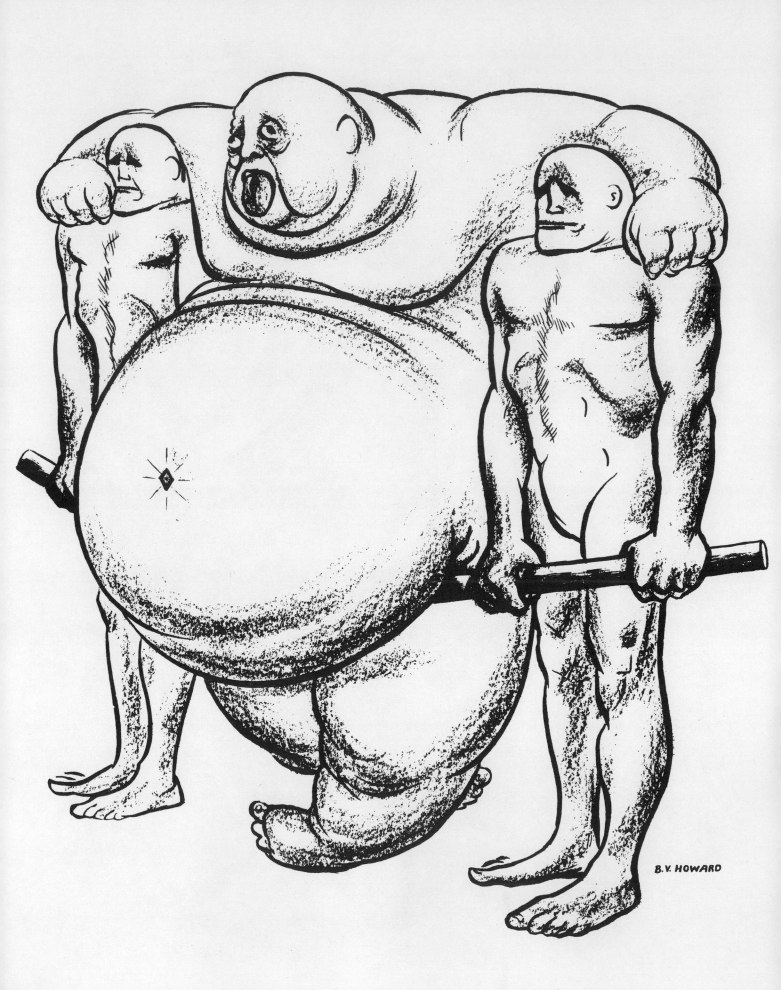

"... whether Capitalism in its present form is to continue."
Franklin D. Roosevelt

Savagery in Pictures

I have as little to do with the pictures in Americana as anyone; I like them probably as anyone else, which means that I like some enormously, some a little, and some none at all. I think the artists who draw for Americana have the same tendency as the artists who draw for The New Yorker, the exhibitions at the Art Students' League, and the comic strips: they like to draw fat ladies, the artists of The New Yorker making them funny, the students making them representative, and the Americana boys making them grotesque and ugly. Sometimes this ugliness seems to me to be pointless. Sometimes not.

The Editor of The Nation thinks the whole magazine "unpleasantly sadistic," judging by last month's issue, and he's probably right. Most artists I have met (and I've met a lot of them, including the best of the lot and probably the worst) make a lot of drawings which aren't saleable as magazine covers; there are thousands of pornographic Japanese prints about (very dull, too, I find most of them) and there are Goyas and Rowlandsons and Beardsleys which give you a shock at first sight—and are damn well meant to give you a shock. There is George Grosz—a co-editor of this magazine—who has stripped the clothes from some foul-looking human beings so that, after you have looked at them for a long time, it is rather unpleasant to go out in the streets, for fear you will see as clearly as he does. (The sensation passes; we are not artists and not as sensitive as Grosz; we compromise with the clothes and are charming.)

The depiction, in line, of cruelty isn't a crime, if the sketch is well done. It does not even prove that the artist takes exceptional pleasure in cruelty and is a sadist himself. All it proves is that in general magazines print pictures which are pleasing or pleasingly grotesque; and when a magazine prints pictures which aren't, artists naturally send to it the things they cannot get printed elsewhere. Twenty years ago we should have been called lechers for printing any nude not quite as demure as September Morn; today it is hardly worth bothering about.

However, I will suggest to the editors of Americana that they reform. No more sadism. Only pretty pictures of sweet communists welcoming Trotsky back from exile; sweet capitalists washing the feet of the ten million unemployed, and sweet editors of liberal magazines smiling broadly at love triumphant.

—*Gilbert Seldes.*

FORECAST OF THE FALL ELECTIONS.

MYTHOLOGY

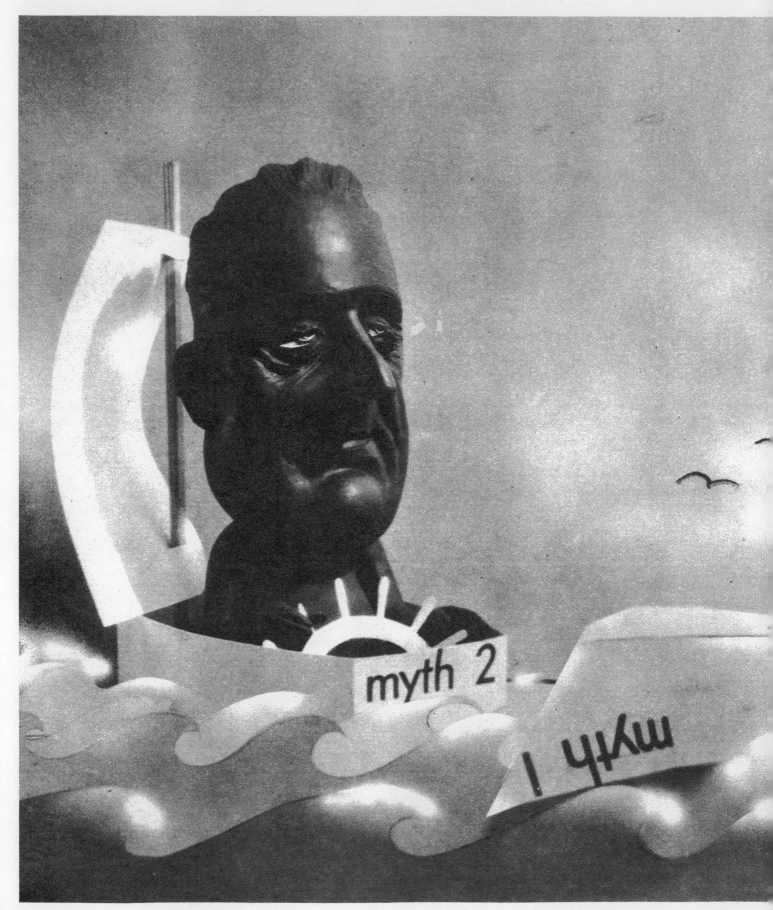

The Roosevelt yacht, MYTH THE SECOND, seems to be floundering successully
into those deep waters where Mr. Hoover's MYTH THE FIRST has already come to grief.

LET'S SHOOT ALL THE OLD MEN

Let us shoot all the men over fifty, over forty—to hell with it, the editors of *Americana* will line themselves up before any wall, if the others are willing and make it all the men over twenty. For God's sake, let us sit upon the ground and tell sad stories of the deaths of kings. Let us leave the Presidency to the young man who, at the age of eight, wrote a biography of Hoover; let us leave exploration to Byron Untiedt, the hero of the Colorado blizzard; let us leave the movies to Jackie Coogan and Jackie Cooper and all the other Jackies and Mitzi Green; let us leave violin playing to the half-grown and literature to the half-wits. Let us have young Randolph Churchill as prime minister of Great Britain and Mihai as King of the Balkans. The only respectable people of the last decade have all been under thirty—the racketeers. Let no old man escape.

Let us shoot* Nicholas Murray Butler for being so damned liberal when he could be such a good conservative and George Jean Nathan for saying "the smile of the Gish girl is a bit of happiness trembling on a bed of death" and Charles Curtis for trying so hard to be Vice-President twice, and the editors of the Nation and the New Republic for not having a million circulation between them and Charlie Chaplin for not making pictures and all the other people in Hollywood for making pictures. Let us shoot the editors of the New Yorker for being so urbane and the editors of the New Masses for being so angry and Alexander Hamilton for being the best secretary of the Treasury before Andrew Mellon.†

Let us shoot all the Pulitzer prize winners and all authors of books circulated by the book clubs and George S. Kaufman for helping in one bad play and Alexander Woollcott for making life difficult for us by occasionally deviating into sense and Al Capone for getting caught and Admiral Byrd for taking the name of Charles V. Bob off his map of the Polar wastes, and the makers of all package cigarets for those damnable half-packed cigarets in the corners of the package and the Woolworth management for going up to twenty cents and all apple-venders who sell chocolate and the keepers of cordial shops.

Let us awake in the chill dawn and shoot Calvin Coolidge and Babe Ruth and the people who make crippled soldiers listen to Kate Smith and the producers of second-string vaudeville and Mayor McKee who shut up the burlesque houses and Macy's for insisting that it's smart to be thrifty and those who don't kiss, but tell, and all radio announcers and Bernard Shaw and the congressmen who urged the bonus army to come to Washington and General MacArthur and, for God's sake, Pat Hurley and all economists except Maynard Keynes and Babsons and Francis Garvan and the editors of Vanity Fair, if any, and the fire-salers on Fifth Avenue and all drivers with repeal signs on their motor cars and the men who put toothpicks outside Theodore Dreiser's door and Theodore Dreiser and the publishers of dull smutty books and Alfred Knopf for his clean edition of Lady Chatterly's Lover and Benarr MacFadden for yelling for a dictator and everyone who says Nerts and the manufacturers of toilet paper who scare the life out of you in their ads.

Let us buy sawed-off shotguns and subcalibre machine guns and hire a car and cry havoc and shoot down crowds of people for being in crowds and let us have scouting parties to creep into the offices of all architects who built Park Avenue apartments and the manufacturers of all-metal rowing machines. Let us have sniping practise for all employers who threaten their men with hell-fire if they do not vote for Foster and let us lay mines under both houses of Congress and let us have firing squads for the Jumping Juliuses of Washington, Klein and Barnes, and let us do something about Professor Irving Fisher, Professor Irving Babbitt, and the editor of the Bookman.

Let us shoot John Barrymore and Al Jolson for being bad movie actors instead of good stage actors and let us mow down Brinkley of Kansas and all the people who will vote for him and let us have a holocaust of all the people who went to the theatre with Jimmie Walker with single bullets left over for the Hofstader committee and let us shoot George Gershwin for getting out sheet music in limited editions and let us leave alive only the southern judge who declared that the depression was not an act of God, and a hundred million bourgeois who never got their names in print.

—THE VIGILANTES.

*To avoid prosecution or the charge of incitement to justice, the words "with confetti" must be understood after the word "shoot" throughout.

†Mistake here; he was shot.

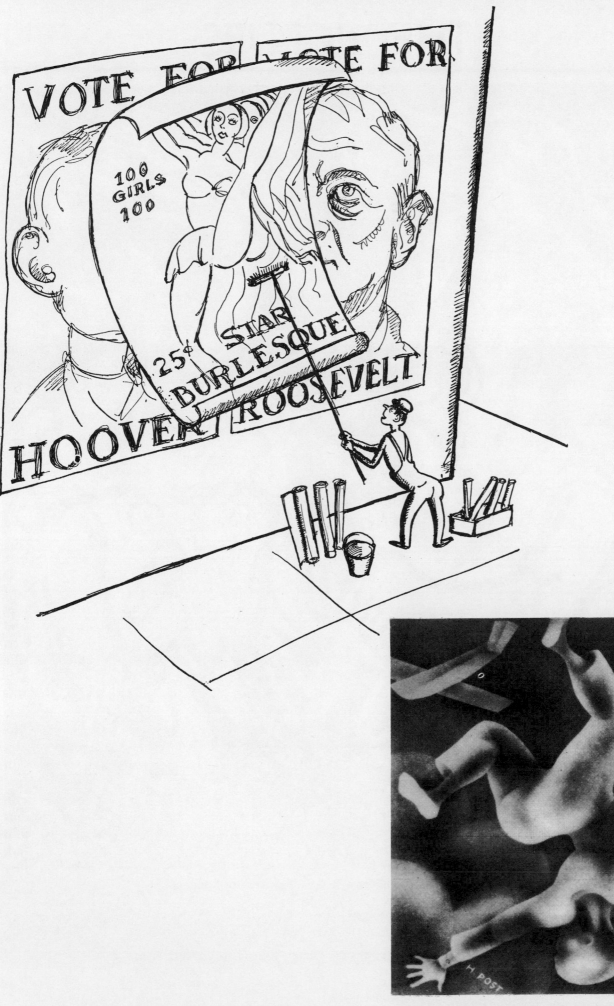

The Forgotten Man, after the election

THE VICTORS

"It was a tough fight, Nancy old kid, but now we got four years to sleep it off in."

Veteran of 30 years in Congress, Texan John Nance
Garner (1869–1967) was FDR's running mate in 1932.

THE NATION

So what?

TEN THOUSAND DOLLARS REWARD!

In its endless zeal for the purification of American life, this Magazine will pay Ten Thousand Dollars for evidence leading to the apprehension and conviction of all the following Fugitives from Justice, corruptors of Society, and Gallows-Cheaters.

Sufficient particulars are given for each Wanted Person. If found, notify nearest police department by telegraph, and keep victim closely guarded.

WARNING! Some of these men are desperate! Beware of concealed weapons!

CALVIN COOLIDGE

•

Has already served one full term and part of another. A thin kind of man. Stock promoter and operator under the Blue Sky Law. Congenitally loquacious. Indicted of selling prosperity to America under false pretences. Guilty of extreme and unnatural cruelty. Will be identified by a copy of his own article in the Saturday Evening Post saying, "our social fabric has remained intact and our long-established methods of relief have proved adequate to meet the strain." Known to have been friendly with Ohio gang, now trailing with Baby-face Hoover.

NOT WANTED IN WASHINGTON!

HERBERT HOOVER (ALIAS "THE CHIEF", "THE PRESIDENT", "THE GREAT ENGINEER")

•

Wanted for deportation to Belgium; high crimes and misdemeanors in office. Has escaped sentence for breach of promise during last three years by claiming immunity, act of God, and European entanglements. Can be approached freely as doesn't know what it's all about. Usually asleep, and can be identified by mutters of "No dole" and "the worst is over." Should be woken gently. Said to be wanted in Iowa. All other states waive rights.

JOSEF von STERNBERG

•

Will be found in company of Marlene Dietrich. Cannot be surprised, as has been in Hollywood, but must be taken in full fight. Wanted in California for spoiling a beautiful actress; wanted in Brooklyn for misappropriation of vons. Wanted generally for abuse of locomotives. Wanted in Soviet Russia for having looked too long at China Express. Wanted in Hollywood for tendency to become a bore. Must not be allowed near an expense account while under surveillance.

FRANKLIN (ALIAS FRANK, ALIAS NOT SO FRANK) ROOSEVELT

•

Wanted since last January for undermining confidence by spreading report that "the American system of economics and government is everlasting." Wanted in Albany for drawing salary without doing his work. Wanted in Milwaukee for making beer. Wanted as a *pis aller* (alias: faute de mieux) in various parts of the country. Will not show fight when surrounded, but look out for dodges. If operating under an alias, can be identified by prolonged stuttering over the word "bonus" which, if pronounced at all, sounds like bonehead. Not one of the old Roosevelt gang, but dangerous at large.

THE APPEAL TO REASON

LET CONGRESS TURN THE FACTORY CHIMNEYS OF AMERICA INTO PENTHOUSES
FOR THE POOR

"My friends, the peak of the depression is definitely behind us."

HAPPY DAYS ARE HERE AGAIN

The dullwits and the defeatists who thought that America was through, not because we had lost a few billion dollars, but because we had lost the capacity to think, or estimate the thoughts of others, are now revising their opinion. In the past eight weeks, an Idea has been exploded in the big furry ear of America, and the way America jumped has proved a miracle of youthfulness and mental alertness.

The Idea, in its prime, was that the world is so full of a number of machines, I am sure we should all be as happy as Americans. The one thing this country always needed was a touch of the tropics, long lazy afternoons with everything provided by bounteous nature. The Idea promised us just that. It sounded different, because the words and names had all come from economists who had completed their work twenty years ago; fundamentally, it meant Good Times Coming. There was a rumor of a little work to be done — but no more than the average highpower executive can get through between golf games. Beyond that everything was rosy.

An Idea as big as that implies that its owners must have some sense of proportion. Yet they are so incompetent that they were unable to present it to America as a promise of Happy Days. They meant to say the words, perhaps; but something got twisted in their throats and what issued was an ugly threat. The one thing they had to offer, leisure and happiness, issued as Starvation.

Whereupon two things occurred, almost simultaneously. The Idea filled page one of all the newspapers and everyone began shouting that it was all wrong, by several decimal places. Manufacturers of motor cars, on hearing that they could manufacture more and better motor cars with less and less people, denied the premises and said they were going to manufacture more and more motor cars, probably with less people. They didn't like to mention it, but they meant that they would keep right on making a profit out of their cars, which, oddly enough, the Idea had overlooked.

At the same time, a lot of people who hadn't the plant to manufacture motor cars, decided that the Idea was the Light of the World and several of them wrote to Time comparing the original owner of the Idea with Jesus Christ, while the rest were panting to be led out of bondage by a man named Moses.

The Big Men were pathetic because the moment anyone said, Look, this is going to happen, they hadn't the courage or the intellect to say, No, because we are going to make something else happen. The little ones were merely pitiable, because they were willing to accept even the threat of Starvation, if it sounded authoritative, in preference to the indecisive mutterings of a lot of people in Washington.

Our salutations to Technocracy. It muddled itself so in its first public appearance that it will take ten years to explain what it did not mean. It supplied Will Rogers with material for three telegrams to the New York Times. It frightened the men in Wall Street. And it showed how brightly, competently, intelligently, and fearlessly, Americans can accept a new Idea, even in the years of the locust.

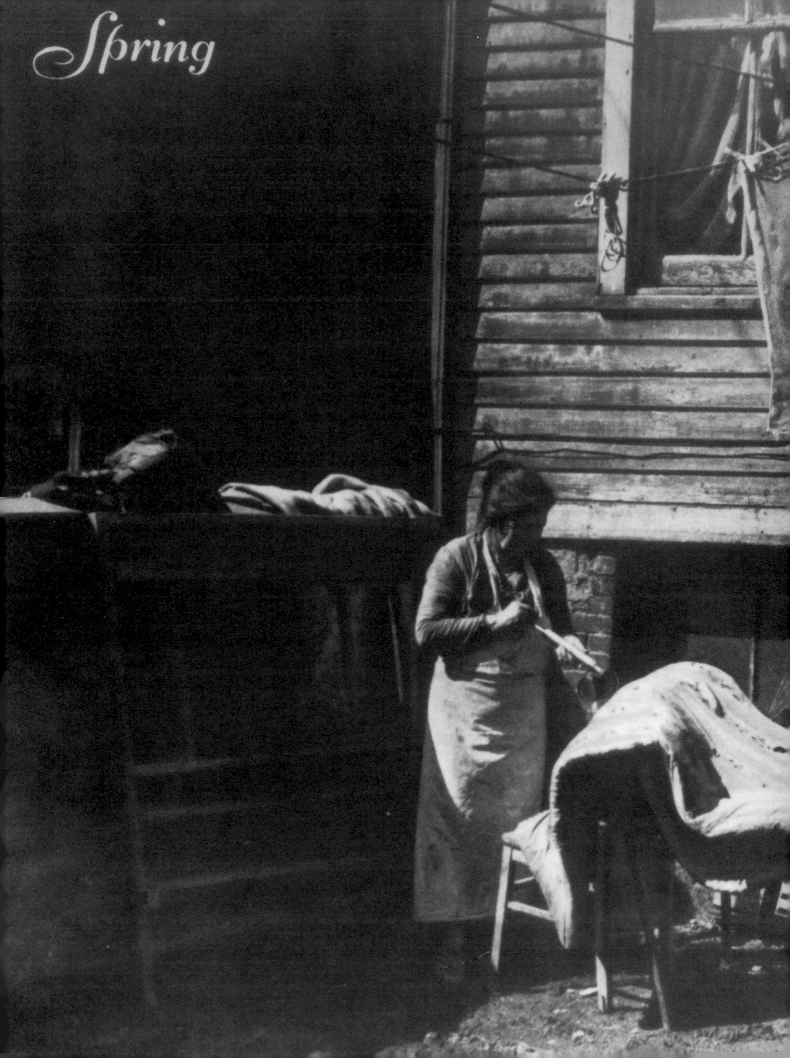

Spring

INFLATION

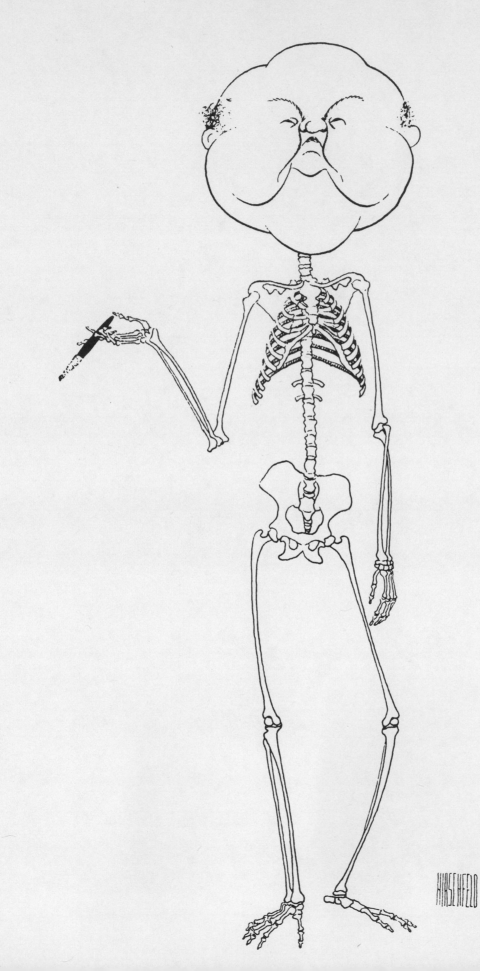

CONTROLLED INFLATION

THE GREAT DELANO!

"Sh-h! don't applaud too loudly; he's liable to drop everything."

BUT IS THIS CONSTRUCTIVE CRITICISM?

By CHARLES D. YOUNG

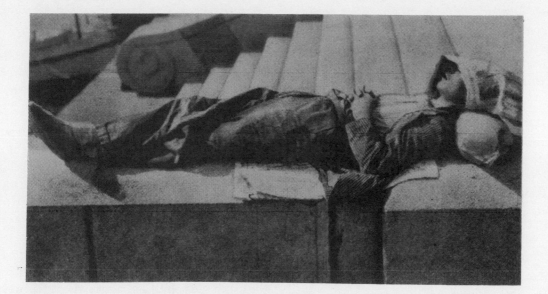

Americans are proverbially fickle towards their public men. They took poor Hoover's name off the Hoover Dam when that pathetic exile had already been safely banished to California. Witness the ugly gloating that followed in the wake of Jimmie Walker and remember the pathetic finish of that erstwhile apostle the late Woodrow Wilson.

We take occasion therefore to anticipate the eventual and unavoidable fate of Franklin Delano Roosevelt. His regime is still young and he had the good fortune to take control after a completely negative and colorless administration. His demonstrations at the white house have so far been enormously dramatic and he has, for the time at least, captured the imagination of the people.

Let us suppose, however, that the industrial recovery act fails to bring about those tangible results which all of us are so devoutly anticipating; let us further imagine that next winter finds our last shreds of optimism on the wane. In that event the very drastic and forceful maneuvers which are at present so vigorously applauded at the newsreel theatres will seem like the most hideous kind of pretentious play-acting.

If this should come to pass, and it seems not entirely impossible, his apologists, that is, the job-holders under him, will have occasion to learn an old lesson over again. It will be vain for them to point out the stupendousness of the task confronting him and their explanations no matter how justified and reasonable will be greeted with fierce cat-calls.

In France a Briand could fall from grace twenty times and find himself restored to power after each seemingly final dismissal. In England a man's chances for recovering public favor end only with the termination of his life. It is different with us. Woe to the man whose pedestal begins cracking. It was a piece of great good fortune that lifted Lincoln out of this life before he too became a persecuted and disillusioned man. Historians have gingerly indicated that his popularity was waning at the time of his tragic death.

Imagine what would have become of Harding and recall the sour jibes that were beginning to be flung at Coolidge shortly before he died.

Roosevelt has one distinct advantage, of course, there happens to be no other man at the present moment who could more adequately fill his precarious job and of this the entire country happens to be aware. He is an astute manipulator of public attention and less given to tawdry political stratagems than any other public man in the land, with the exception perhaps, of Alfred Emanuel Smith.

In any event, he is subject to the most treacherous task-master in the whole world, the mobs which now trample each other to death, to get a glimpse of him.

Dictatorship—American Plan

By DON LANGAN

THEME—STARS AND STRIPES FOREVER

Announcer:

Greetings, ladies and gentlemen of the radio audience. That inspiring march means it's Government time again. Before we get to the Nation's business tonight Miss Etta Mermaid of the Tip Top Club will entertain with a little number written especially for this occasion.

"Pay Up Your Taxes from Your Ol' Wool Sock An' Smile—Smile—Smile" (MISS MERMAID)

(Orchestra Reprise)

Announcer:

Now, Everybody, are you set? Here goes the magic carpet. To the President's Study! Hang on! Okay, America!

(Wheeeeeeeeeeee)

The President:

Good evening, my friends. It is a pleasure to be with you in another of our Wednesday evening legislative sessions. For those of you who missed the opening broadcast last week let me say again that the Government of this great country of ours has gone back into the hands of the people, where it belongs. In accordance with this new deal we shall meet through the wonderful medium of radio once each week for the purpose of formulating the laws of our land. The power of enactment and administration of all laws has been bestowed on me by the Congress, and in turn I pass it on to you, remaining in the capacity of counsel and director. It is up to you and me to use this vast power for the greatest good of the greatest number. As announced last week, everybody listening in is privileged to enter this con—great endeavor—to set our ship of state on an even keel. If you have in mind a law which you earnestly believe should be enacted sit down, write it out in twenty words—no more, no less—and mail it to the station to which you are listening. Your law to be valid for consideration must be written on the back of a Postal Savings Receipt, or facsimile thereof, and postmarked not later than midnight of next Friday. Each week I will announce the winning law and the author's name. The prize, as formerly announced, is a three-day trip to your nation's capital, all expenses paid *or* one year's relief from income tax payment. You take your choice. In case of ties duplicate prizes will be awarded.

Now, to announce this week's winner.
(Fanfare)

Mrs. Wellington Klaber of Goose Creek, Oklahoma, is the lucky la—citizen. Congratulations, Mrs. Klaber! The law proposed by Mrs. Klaber, to be enacted immediately reads as follows:

Vacuum cleaner salesmen and college boys selling magazines calling on washday will be liable to fine or imprisonment or both.
(Fanfare)

According to the rules of our meetings, my friends, this law goes into effect at midnight tonight by Presidential decree. I know you will be interested to hear that upwards of two million letters were received following last week's broadcast. Both Houses of Congress, aided by an army of clerks, have worked night and day reading and indexing them. As you were advised, the procedure is as follows: Each Representative reviews the letters from his district, sorting out the possibilities for further discussion with the Senators. One law for each state is decided upon. Decision, in accordance with Presidential decree, must be reached by Wednesday morning. Following delivery of the 48 laws, your President with the help of his cabinet, chooses the winning law to be announced each evening.

All of us here in Washington are looking forward to this week's mailing. Do your part toward the rebuilding of your nation. Go out *now* and procure a Postal Savings receipt at your nearest Post Office. If this is absolutely impossible, then make a facsimile of one. On the back of it write *your* law in twenty words—no more, no less—and mail without delay. Remember, midnight Friday is the deadline. Good night, my friends.
(Orchestra Reprise)

Announcer:

You have just heard the President announce the winner of last week's legislative action. Next Wednesday evening, at Government Time, the President will again speak to you, and announce another winner. Be sure to tune in. Until then, good night. This is Horton Spokenwire speaking.

Station Announcer:

This is the LIBERTY . . . BROADCASTING SYSTEM.

(Fade Out in 10 seconds)
(Orchestra playing "AMERICA")
W.A.L. NEW YORK

WASHINGTON AIR WAVES

"Remember, my friends, it is YOUR strength, YOUR pluck and YOUR capacity for constructive thinking that can pull us out of all our present difficulties!"

The camel passes through the eye of the needle

President Roosevelt brought burly General Hugh S. Johnson (1882–1942) to Washington to head the National Recovery Administration (NRA). Designed as part of an emergency measure passed in mid-1933 to bolster industry, the bureau developed a blanket code regulating fair competition, as well as codes guiding wage and hours policies for individual industries. Johnson made the blue eagle the NRA symbol, and ordered it prominently displayed on products, shops, and even households (unlike most other magazines, Americana did not add the eagle to their masthead page).

THE DESCENT FROM SINAI

".. when he found that they had made unto themselves a calf of gold."

G. O. P.

Seidenstuecker

DECLINE OF A FAMOUS NORTH AMERICAN PACHYDERM

Excerpt from a History of the United States — 1983 A.D.

By the beginning of 1933 and particularly at the time of Franklin D. Roosevelt's inauguration, the American people were ripe for a paternalistic government. The preceding years of halting indecision and blind groping for a way out of the economic stagnation by the Republican (Reactionary) Party leaders had made the populace ready to support tangible action of any kind whatsoever. Their attitude presents an excellent study in mass temperament. Mr. Roosevelt immediately closed every bank in the country, thus paralyzing for more than a week the meagre trade that was left. During ensuing weeks he renounced the gold standard, impairing the credit of the people, and went so far as to refuse payment in gold on the Government indebtedness, although such payment was expressly stipulated in the securities themselves; he tempered the riotous feeling among the farmers by proclaiming a policy of inflated prices at a time when thirteen millions were unemployed and largely without income of any kind; he raised taxes; he plunged into the turmoil of European intrigue, security pacts and consultative commitments, abandoning the policy of American isolation for which politicians had oratorically bled and died. The American People applauded every move and followed him with the fervent faithfulness of myopic sheep, and even gave him by public subscription a swimming pool. Playing politics with a skilful hand, he forestalled any wide tolerance of questioning or disapproval from the more courageous by interspersing his sudden moves toward dictatorial power with sops to a hungry people. To the populace at large he gave beer of 3.2 alcoholic content—it lulled them into meek silence. To the powerful industrialists who might have blocked some of his more paternalistic moves he gave a business partnership with the government—assuring them a continued existence amidst crumbling values. In the summer of that year. . . .

d. b. l.

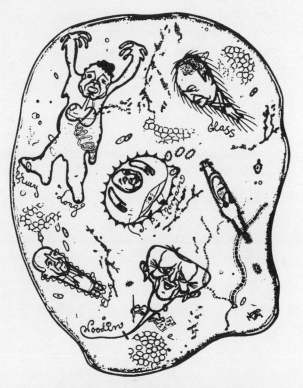

A drop of perspiration from the forehead of F. D. Roosevelt

WOODIN* NICKELS
AND BIG BUCKS

THE NATIONS' BANKS, even more consistently than its churches, had been designed and built in the solid architectural style of classical temples. The Depression quickly destroyed all faith in these sanctuaries for the ritual exchange of money. Between the stock market crash of October 29, 1929, and the end of 1933, more than 9,000 banks failed in the United States, a loss of about $2.5 billion to depositors and creditors. These failures caused the stock of money to fall by one third, the largest decline in the country's monetary history. A sudden drop in January 1933 marked the beginning of the third and most severe banking crisis since the crash. Rumors that the new president would devalue produced a gold drain and a new rash of bank failures. On March 4 in his inaugural address, President Roosevelt assured the country that there was nothing to fear but fear itself. The following night he proclaimed a four-day nationwide bank holiday and prohibited gold payments and foreign exchange transactions until further notice; he later extended the suspension through Friday, March 10. Reopening of sound banks the following week was contingent upon licensing by the Federal Reserve System or state banking authorities (several thousand banks never reopened). Thus the first week of Roosevelt's Hundred Days was the most extraordinary week in recent history. There was no money and the temple doors were shut.

*William H. Woodin (1868–1936), Secretary of the Treasury in the new cabinet, was an amateur musician, composer of the "Franklin Delano Roosevelt March." A cartoon in the April 1933 issue of the humorous magazine *Life* (the name would be sold in 1936 to Henry Luce) showed two office boys pointing to a bouncer outside the Secretary's frosted door. One boy explains, "He's supposed to throw out everyone who wisecracks about Woodin nickels."

•

Theory of American Business:
Millions are made by fools like me,
but only God can make a depression.

•

What this country needs is five cents.

•

Political Motto: It's smart to be shifty.

SOUND AND FURY

"Here's to the sound background of our country's economic structure!"

THE LAST CENT

THE LAST MILLION

"Listen, old man, what do they mean by the gold standard?"

The Rope Around Grandfather's Neck

With sublime unconcern for that delightful commodity—confidence—the Senate of the United States is conducting an investigation into, of all things, the causes of the depression. This isn't the first time the Senate has shown itself aware of the depression—the other time occurred in 1931, and individual Senators have, from sheer weakness to withstand the pressure of newspapers and bonus marchers, several times brought in bills which indicated that something had happened to them as well (or rather as ill) as to the rest of us. The current scrutiny of affairs is more important because it is a little unfriendly in tone. Mr. Pecora, digging into the consciences of the testifiers, seems not to give a damn for their private feelings and the Senate hasn't been exactly friendly. The chief victim, so far, is Charles E. Mitchell, of the National City Bank, who has the outstanding merit of having predicted the crash six months before it came and the equally outstanding demerit of having protected himself a little more sedulously than he protected the public good.

The misfortune which we will suffer, on account of these disclosures, is going to make the past three years seem like jam and cake. It isn't a question of losing confidence in our bankers; any banker who has enjoyed the actual confidence of Americans lately is a dead banker or a retired banker. The danger lies in another direction. With its customary ballyhoo, the Senate will turn up a series of villains, and we are all in the mood for finding a scapegoat. The moment that is done, and our appetite for revenge is satisfied, we will forget that the combined villainy of all the bankers and brokers, the stupidity of Lee Higginson multiplied by the unscrupulousness of Insull—all of these together are not enough to account for what fell upon us.

In a word, the errors of individuals are nothing in comparison with the faults of a system. We are trying to run a rope around grandfather's neck—but the noose is going to slip, and before we know it we'll find it round our own.

—Gilbert Seldes

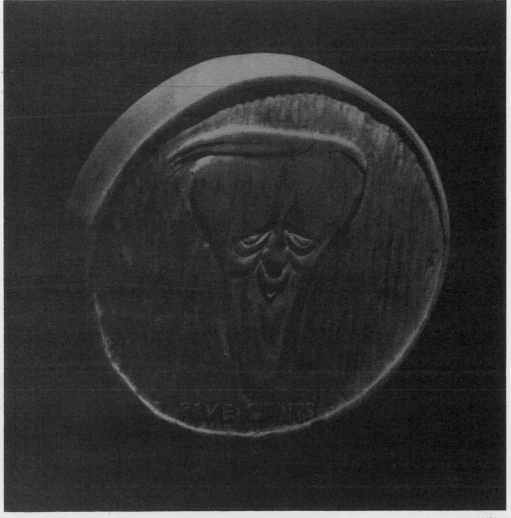

THE WOODIN NICKEL

Hirschfeld

HAUNTED HOUSES

BANKERS ARISE

By KENNETH BURKE

Without prosperity, we have lost more than our jobs and our incomes. We have lost our very characters. We are mere mournful zeros sitting around the house. We are slippers-and-bathrobe at the wrong hours, a hollow function-of-taking-the-children-to-school.

Who is to rescue us? Guided by history, we turn to the bankers for relief. Salvation must come primarily from the promoters of invesment, else history is a strumpet. Runners of bucket shops, sharpers, peddlers of gold bricks, confidence men,

backers of crooked real estate projects, swindlers plugging for the construction of ten thousand miles of railroad through the heart of Tierre del Fuego—it is these men who gave us our great commercial exaltations of the past, and it is they alone who can bring us another such exaltation in the future. It is they who can reach beneath the nation's pillows, grope to the bottom of old socks, unfasten floorboards, releasing for wholesome speculative purposes the sums now languishing in darkness. These men can bring back that very real and exhilarating prosperity

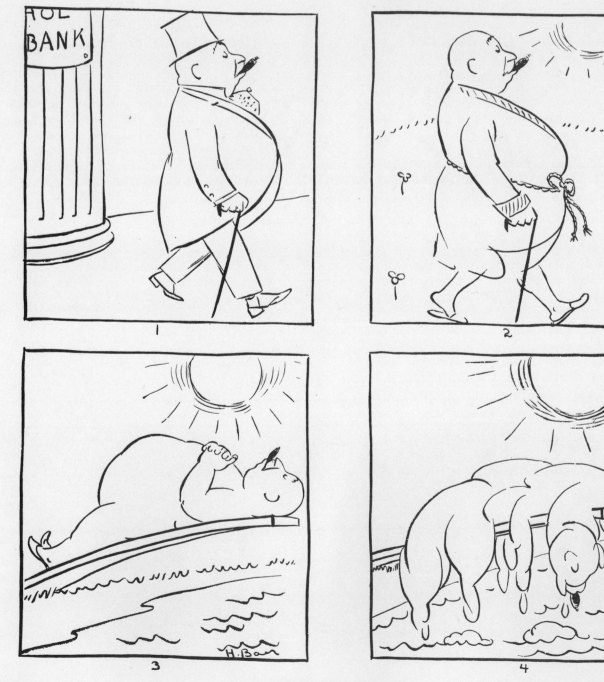

which is the *true meaning* of bankruptcy. And it is the *bankers alone* who can restore our faith in these crooks whose shady deals have, in the past, brought such glory and feverish activity to the State.

Bankers, arise! In the heat of our economic anguish, we have wronged you at times. We have even blamed you for the collapse that is now upon us, saying that you led us into all kinds of wildcat speculations. But where would our ten years of prosperity have come from, had you not promoted precisely these same wildcat speculations? Forgive us what we said in rashness. We see now that, by the gentle, Christlike wheedling of your investment-affiliates, you lured forth the savings of the well-to-do, turning these funds into all sorts of vast constructive ventures, and so letting the manna of work drop upon our people.

What the world pants for now is precisely another bad-invesment—a worse one by far than we have ever known since Ferdinand and Isabella financed some thieves and a madman on a speculative trip to the East by going West (a particular kind of inconsistancy that has plagued us ever since, so that everything is the opposite of what it should be, and we are starving because there is too much food).

Bankers! We hereby propose that you float a bond issue to *pave the Sahara Desert with a mixture of wheat, steel, cement, corn, and automobile parts.* In the first place, this would be as bad as any investment made in South America during the last ten years, and so should be expected to have as stimulating an effect upon our trade as those did. Not only would this project dispose of our entire exportable surplus, but twenty years would be required to get the paving job completed, and so it would be twenty years before investors expected the books of the Sahara Paving Corporation to show a profit. And, *since we could not prove ourselves bankrupt for twenty years, and since prosperity is that state preceeding the state wherein one discovers that one is bankrupt,* it follows that, *with the help of this great key promotion, we should enjoy twenty years of the purest financial exaltation.*

Not only would we dump into the Sahara, in the way of wheat, steel, cement, corn, and automobile parts, greater enormities of wealth than all the combined armies and navies of the world could take from us by force, but the *radiations* from this one sublime speculative source would be endless. The people's wages by a sweet going-back-and-forth, would stimulate all kinds of subsidiary industries. We should feel again the call to move into remote areas of the world, bringing new regions within the enchantment of our commercial understanding, going further perhaps into deepest Africa, where people have mistakenly sung and danced since the times of pre-history, but where we should draft them for work in the mines and on rubber plantations, and for any other kinds of enterprise we might think it educational to found there (and so we should solve for them at last an unemploy-ment problem which has existed there since the human race was born).

We might live in palaces, with a thousand highly refined mechanical servants in each. We might saunter through Babylonic gardens erected upon walls of steel and masonry. We might step into little whisking things that took us in a flash to areas once thought completely inaccessible. I could go on endlessly, picturing the fabulous material translation of this country that could take place were you, by a benevolent bond-issue for paving the Sahara, to enable us to cast out from our borders a large portion of the wealth which we are now equipped to produce.

Bankers, Arise! This is our system, and we love it, and we call upon you to organize some kindly swindle that will help the Highest Court of our Land to protect and perpetuate our institutions. Promote the Greatest Bubble, the mightiest and economically the Most Invigorating Default in Human History, the Paving of the Sahara. Thereby, gentlemen, *the national curse of a national surplus will be removed.* And as for those who now ask why a surplus is a curse, and who insist, in stupid brutal ways, that the economic order should be changed to make a national surplus into a national benefit, *they have betrayed the fact that they do not know the difference between right and wrong, and thus they cannot appreciate the sanctity of the institutions upon which the American system (I said system) is founded.*

BANK INVESTIGATION

BANK HOLIDAY

Atget

AMERICAN UNTOUCHABLES

"CAME THE DAWN"

SUB-TREASURY — WALL STREET

THE LAST COURSE

THIS COCK-EYED WORLD

As the first issue of *Americana* went to press in February 1932, delegates from 59 nations gathered in Geneva for the opening session of the World Disarmament Conference convened by the League of Nations. Overt skepticism was the prevailing attitude toward the conference; the Japanese invasion of Manchuria had proceeded unchecked for the past five months, despite a League investigative committee, and in January China had to plead with the League to halt Japanese bombing of civilians. On January 7, 1932, President Hoover's Secretary of State Henry L. Stimson, soon to take over as chairman of the U.S. delegation in Geneva, sent identical firm notes to China and Japan stating the American position. Just as the conference opened the U.S. and Great Britain ordered their fleets to the China coast to monitor the tense situation caused by the landing of Japanese marines in Shanghai.

America followed the war in China through the broadcasts of war correspondent Floyd Gibbons (1887–1939), noted for his eyepatch and his staccato delivery, said to average 217 words per minute. Criticizing his coverage of the Japanese invasion as a purposeful exploitation of human suffering, *Vanity Fair* awarded Gibbons their "Nomination for Oblivion" in June 1932, along with Adolf Hitler.

Despite his honor from *Vanity Fair*, Adolf Hitler did not disappear; by November his caricature was on the cover of that elegant magazine. On January 30, the elderly German president Paul von Hindenburg appointed Hitler chancellor of Germany. A fire in the Reichstag on February 27 said to be the work of Communists provided Hitler with an excuse to take emergency measures. He assumed absolute power in March and immediately launched a systematic persecution of Jews, intellectuals, and political opponents.

Benito Mussolini (1883–1945) had been absolute dictator of Italy for a decade when *Americana* began. His architectural triumphs of the early 1930s made him the subject of caricature in the democratic press. Nordley's inspired drawing for the January 1933 issue of *Americana* (p. 103) may refer to the Mussolini column in the heart of Rome's new Fascist forum; Il Duce had recently opened a stadium in Carrara marble topped with 25-foot nudes.

"The greatest show on earth, ladies and gentlemen, featuring Handsome Herbie, the human target who keeps on taking it and comes back for more every time. Above him, we have the Skeleton Man from India, with the goat of England. Next to him, we have the Mechanical Marvel from Russia who hasn't had a leg to stand on in years. In the center we have La Belle France, the sword swallowing lady with the big bank account. On her left squats

SIDE-SHOW

Handsome Adolph, the tattooed man. Next to him, you behold Scott MacDonald with a ball-bearing neck. From the back he's Labor; from the front he's Capital. And finally, take a good squint at the bold boy of the Apennines, Signor Mussolini, the world's most distinguished fire-eater. Step inside, Ladies and Gentlemen, this is a continuous performance."

A Tour of the World In a Thousand Words

By M. R. WERNER

Reading from East to West, we take off from Japan, where peasants are selling their daughters for fish, and the tin soldiers of the Mikado are encouraging the assassination of the opposition, while they bite off slices of Manchuria and try to digest the Chinese bandits. By slow stages through country overrun by poverty-stricken, flood-bereft, Japanese-raped, corruption-ridden, and communist-exploited Chinese people, we arrive in Siberia, where there is one dried duck per twenty million of the population, and where the *wagon-restaurant* rapidly becomes *nyet*. (There's gold in them thar hills!)

Eventually, one reaches Moscow, that Oriental capital of the latest thing on earth, where the plaster is falling into the greasy soup of three million people, as the houses decay and man multiplies. Here Marx speaks only to Stalin, and Stalin tells it to Voroshilov, whose Red Army stands sternly ready to shoot peasants who demand rubber boots which do not exist, for grain which they have fondly raised. The Kremlin barricades its doors from the Japanese on the East, and the Franco-Polish-Czecho-Slovakian-Rumanian combine on the West, whilst the low price of wheat and lumber in the world markets makes the Five Year Plan eternal, and the immortal pee-pul eat rations that would have made even a British Tommy revolt.

Waving goodbye to the land of Lenin and the spirit of the brotherhood of man, we arrive in Poland, where people dance in and out of dictatorships in the Danzig corridor to keep the courage of Pilsudski from getting into the trained fingers of Paderewski, swearing silently that Poles never will be free--from France and Soviet Russia, and Germany, a neighbor, glares and does not like the number of consonants which have been injected into its language by the Treaty of Versailles.

From here a side trip is optional to Sweden, the land of the late Kreuger, whose commitments caught up with his hopes, whilst he found himself in the act of burning up his promissory notes with his own matches. For the first time since Charles XII beggars are to be met frequently in the Gustav Adolfs Torg at Stockholm, where investigators and auditors, like Elliott-Fisher-Remington-Rand hawks, wrangle over the carrion of Kreuger's corpse.

But, perhaps it would be worse to visit Germany, where the Young-Men's-Anti-Jewish-Association-Boy-Scout-Swastikas never get enough of killing communists whom Moscow has forgotten, since the World Depression beat the World Revolution to the goal of despair. Papa Hindenburg holds tight to the arms of his royal rocking chair, whilst frantic burghers looking for sausages and beer see to the right of them the yellowing wrinkles of the ex-Crown Prince, trying to look Kaiser, and to the left Little Adolph trying to be Prime Minister, while his beaters-up try to be little Adolphs.

Flying to Paris, we pass through snarl pockets and drop on to the land of personal liberty, which maintains the largest standing army in the world, where French bourgeois are afraid to buy frigidaires for fear the Germans will take them away from them. Interviewing persons in high governmental circles, we learn that everything would be all right, if only the League of Nations would move to the Palais Bourbon and the U.S. would abandon *la regime sec*. French *rentiers* spit repudiated *bons-bons* when they think of the five billions loaned to the late Tsar, whilst they hire the sons of Grand Dukes as dressmakers and the characters of Dostoevsky as taxi-drivers.

But let us go to the Eternal City, where Mussolini makes the trains run on time without benefit of bandits and the battleships work over time in order to show France that he is Napoleon come back from St. Helena with a castor oil heart. The Pope, delivers sulking encyclicals over his new radio station.

Thence to the deserted Riviera, where the inhabitants cannot decide whether they resent more that the beastly Americans have gone, or that there are a few of them left. To the west lies Spain, where Madrid trembles for fear of Barcelona and both put down revolts in Seville, whilst they shiver that Trotsky from his island will get them if they don't watch out.

Reaching England, we find the graveyard of liberalism, where children coming out of school go straight to the dole, and Gandhi's starvation turns Lancashire impotent, whilst Ramsay MacDonald urges the world to get around one big table.

Crossing the ocean on an empty new liner, we arrive in the United States, where The Depression waves, and where all for the moment is politics. President Hoover appoints a commission to determine whether he is to be or not to be worried for another four years, and Franklin D. Roosevelt sweeps through an unenthusiastic land asking the forgotten man to give him something to remember him by. Farmers spill their milk to the tune of bonus riot calls, and every time Boston sells a carton of shoes, landlords in New York ask their tenants please can't they pay a little rent. Meanwhile, the bootleggers and the Anti-Saloon League pledge undying loyalty to each other, and the Communists cable Moscow for instructions on how to deal with the evident lack of flower beds in Union Square.

We have brought back with us from our travels jaundice—which alone comes in free of duty—and we hire hotel bedrooms from which to jump, for, alas the gas companies still demand a deposit of ten dollars.

MODERN MESSIAHS

MUSSOLINI

STALIN

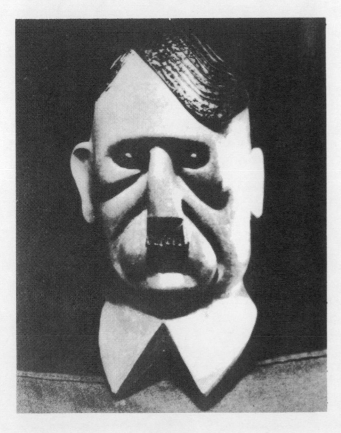

HITLER

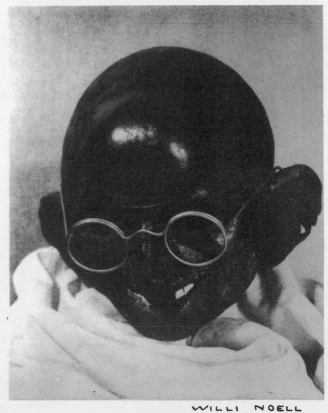

GANDHI

HELLO EVERYBODY!

This is Floyd Gibbons speaking right from the battle front. We have a special treat for you tonight, folks, we are bringing you the last words of the mortally wounded Mr. Joy Hung Low. If you can't hear Mr. Low very clearly, remember this is his first appearance on the air and he may be just a little microphone shy!"

"I wish he could have found someone who spoke a little English."

By Alfred Kubin

THE FORGOTTEN MAN ATTENDS THE PEACE CONFERENCE

All peace conferences, beginning with the one under Ptolemy II in Egypt, were followed by wars of staggering brutality. You are hereby given early warning that the odds are a hundred to one that history will repeat itself. Make your bookings in time for such outlying and unprofitable places on the globe as are likely to be spared in the forthcoming wholesale slaughter. We suggest, tentatively, Spitzbergen, Peru, Iceland and such South American republics as are enjoying wars at the present time. Revolutions and battles south of Mexico have always been conducted with a decent regard for the humanities.

"Won't somebody Puhleeze take that pen away from Mr. Stimson!"

"Don't talk to me about war!"

97

OKAY AMERICA

Turkey Sends Regards

La Belle France Adores You!

Italy Greets You!

These American ladies collected 500,000 signatures endorsing world peace

England is With You!

24-hour marathon-prayer in Pittsburgh to insure world disarmament

Japan Joins You!

BULGARIA IS YOURS HEART + SOUL

Germany Salutes You!

Poland Wants to be REMEMBERED

Moscow is thrilled!

CAMBODIA SENDS LOVE + KISSES

THE MARTIANS

"Looks like the earth is disarming again"

HISTORY FOR THE KIDDIES

20,000 B.C.

2000 B.C.

1000 B.C.

400 B.C.

1500 A.D.

AND SO ON . . . .

BABIES, JUST BABIES

GERMANY

ENGLAND

NEW YORK CITY: The Goldman Band Plays Wagner

POPULAR CONCEPTIONS

THE KINGDOM OF ROUMANIA

ITALY

THE WORLD ECONOMIC CONFERENCE

YOUTH

Student Demonstration in Italy

Student Demonstration in Greece

Student Demonstration in Germany

Student Demonstration in America

THE NEW DEAL

SO FAR, SO GOOD

GAMES

AMERICANA PRESENTS THE HITLER JIG-SAW PUZZLE — Cut out carefully and throw the pieces away

The Goose-Step and Mary Wigman

We have no right to be amazed at the goings on in Germany. Since 1870 the Germans have practiced either the goose-step or interpretive dancing. It is assumed in this country that the so-called rank and file of the German population does not endorse the Nazi excesses. Anyone familiar with the Teutonic spirit must be aware that military drill, martial music, heel-clicking and short, snappy gestures are inseparable from the German ideology.

The only deviation exists among the nudists, the athletic dance groups, the vegetarians and the multifarious nature cranks whose gruesome antics were always an important feature of German life.

It is absurd to refer to the cultural torch-bearers, since no genius can fairly be used as representative of a people, nor can it be reasonably claimed that the artists and writers of Germany have had an overwhelmingly civilizing effect upon the nation.

It is doubtful whether the Germans are capable of purging themselves of their deep-rooted longing for military display and discipline. As long as Hitler maintains some sort of army uniform and sticks to the goose-step, his regime is safe.

The only one who might some day effectively dislodge Adolf, is Mary Wigman, whose girl students are more emphatically masculine than most of the men in the Nazi storm troops.

—*Charles D. Young.*

German modern dancer Mary Wigman (1886–1973) performed in New York during the winter of 1932–33, on a final tour before hostilities with Germany ended her American career.

108

POLITICO-EROTICA

"Oh, Adolf!"

Disraeli

The origin of a famous salute

VOX POPULI: The Spokesman for Heinie

"WORLD RECOVERY—AHOY!"

International Amity

Industrial Recovery

Railroads

Automotive Industry

Disarmament

Housing

Shipping

Return to Fundamentals

Farming

GERMANY SPEAKS

"Aw, stop squawking, she's just a harmless bitch."

The man walking the dog is German President
Paul von Hindenburg (1847–1934).

FASHIONS

THE LATEST THING FROM THE BUG HOUSE

ARYAN ANTICS

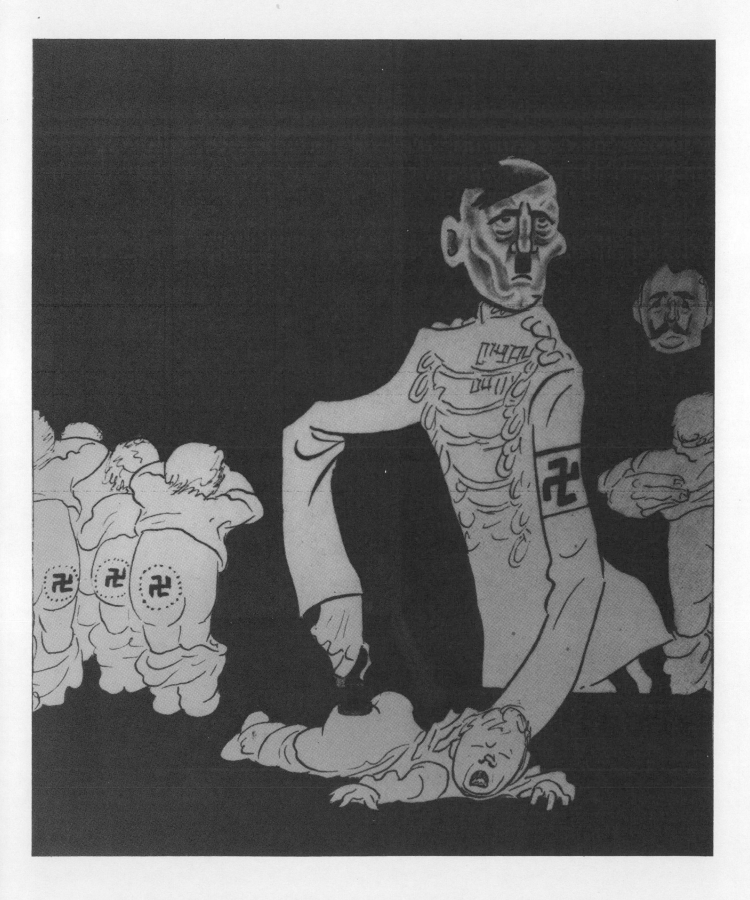

To insure purity of stock, all German infants will be branded at birth with the national symbol

THE THEATER

The Herod figure is another caricature of German
President Paul von Hindenburg (1847–1934).

THE COCK-EYED WORLD

A Chinese Executioner

The bedroom in Zurich where Lenin planned the Russian Revolution

Unretouched Photo of Stalin, smiling

The hangman of Hungary

New York Shop for Hygienic Rubber Goods

That most fiendishly vitriolic caricaturist, Mr. George Grosz

Rasputin posing for his portrait at the studio of the sculptor Agronson in 1914

The gold standard is maintained in the Holy Land

A Russian peasant who witnessed a pogrom, became a Jew—and serves as sexton in a synagogue in Brooklyn

"I don't seem to be able to rid him of his bourgeois preoccupation with food."

COMRAD STALIN INTRODUCES RUSSIA TO THE MACHINE AGE

Americana cover, September 1933

Communism Crashes the Gate

By LAWRENCE DENNIS

Soon we shall be whiskered comrades sipping tea with bejeweled Washington dowagers. Recognition of communist Russia is now a certainty. It has to help save a dying capitalism in America. The first reaction of war bloated American profiteers to Russian communism was that it could be snubbed out of existence. The snubbing, of course, infuriated the poor communists, and even non-communist Russians, who, like most other dumb bunnies have a terrible inferiority complex. Well, to make any dumb bunny a great success, all that is needed is a little stimulation of the old inferiority complex. American capitalists rendered this invaluable service to the cause of communism in Russia and, also, by so doing, saved the economic structure of that country from the evils of over-borrowing and over-rapid industrialization. Not that Russia has not borrowed already too much, especially at home and in Germany; and not that Russia has not industrialized too fast. But the lack of American financial cooperation has necessarily cramped the Russian follies. We saved Russia from the Insulls, Kreugers and Roxies, which was damned decent of us.

Today times are hard and this protective generosity must end. Even without the erg-some reminders of the Technocrats, American capitalists, are beginning to face the alternatives of an early increase in purchasing power or total collapse. Today there are but three ways of increasing purchasing power: (Mr. Rockefeller thought investment for profit in America was a fourth. He thinks different now). Socialistic spending, war, or foreign loans (giving money to foreigners instead of to poor Americans). Now good American capitalists prefer death to a waste of taxpayers' money on public welfare, even if it is the only way to give work to the unemployed, food to the hungry, orders to factories and dividends to investors. As for war, the doings of the veterans and the certainty of a capital levy in our next war, make war most undesirable for capitalists at present.

There remains, therefore, only the foreign loan route back to prosperity. But the trouble here is that all the possible borrowers save Russia are bankrupt and there is no place in the capitalistic world to invest money to produce anything for a profit. (Ask Mr. Rockefeller.) Markets are everywhere glutted with everything any one knows how to produce.

Communist Russia must save capitalist America. There we can invest billions. And it can't be said that Russia is now bankrupt or that investment in Russia will prove unprofitable. We haven't given Russia a chance since the war to borrow and go bankrupt again. And Russia doesn't allow profits.

Some simple soul might ask how we are ever to get our money back from Russia which forbids profits and from which, neither now nor in the future, can anything of importance be exported which is not produced in the United States. Obviously, our only reason for lending to Russia is to dump there a surplus our own people haven't the money to buy. The simple soul must be told not to ask such questions. Foreign loans are not meant to be repaid.

The danger to communism is obvious. Russia will be taking a stiff dose of a capitalist poison, unproductive credit, really to save capitalism and destroy communism. Russia will be obligated to pay interest on money used to relieve suffering in Russia until forced to default. Relieving Russian suffering doesn't produce dollars in New York for capitalist lenders.

With the best foreign governments, the city of New York, the Rockefellers, and the best American railways facing bankruptcy and nearly every bank and insurance company in America insolvent if assets were figured at present market values, the communists want to take a flier at borrowing. They want a chance to show that they can borrow, build white elephants and go bankrupt like regular capitalist folks.

The joke is that some communists are dumb enough to think Russia can beat the capitalist game or that she could borrow and later default without injury. We know how heavy British investments in and trade with Germany before 1914 prevented the World War and cemented the bonds of union between the lenders and borrowers. We also know that is a bank clerk's wife needs an operation and he hasn't the money, a flier in the stock market or on a horse race with temporarily "borrowed" bank funds always brings home the bacon and saves the poor wife. The game that has beaten the New York bankers and the Rockefellers won't beat Stalin and the communists. There is a communist god to prosper their business ventures.

The communists want a Radio City. They won't be happy until they get recognition, loans and trade relations. They must keep up with the Wall Street Jones. They want to dazzle the capitalists rather than merely to weather the storm. They forget that the Russian peasant can stand any amount of privation, just as his ancestors have always done. But the Russian economic machine cannot stand the follies of Wall Street or Detroit or Hoover Dam. Communism is a revolutionary principle. It can survive only as long as it fights and refuses to fraternize with capitalism. Vain and naive leaders want to *achieve* when they should only seek to *survive,* confident in their Marxian dogma of the inevitability of a capitalistic breakdown. They are soon to take the capitalist road to breakdown.

BETROTHALS

"I wonder if she's marrying him for his money."

WHAT THIS COUNTRY NEEDS IS...

SOLUTIONS PROPOSED to solve America's problems burgeoned with the growing perception of a grave world crisis. Offered on various levels, these solutions ranged from Nudism to the Edison dollar (a new monetary unit based on the kilowatt hour suggested during the Technocracy craze late in 1932). Some solutions combined the ludicrous with a subtle menace, such as Technocracy itself (see p. 151), or Huey Long's relentless wooing of voters with slogans like "Beer by Christmas" or "A Chicken in Every Pot." Behind every proposal lay a more serious consideration than ever before of the battling European ideologies — Communism and Fascism.

In *Americana*'s February 1933 issue, shortly before the inauguration of President Roosevelt, Gilbert Seldes complained in an editorial of the

fatuous complacence of our financial magicians who have whisked their napkins off the goldfish bowl of the depression a hundred times in the past three years, crying out "It's gone!" and covering up the consequent confusion, since the damn thing not only refuses to vanish, but actually grows bulkier with every repetition...

It's either the wrong bowl or the wrong trick. By this time the people watching it are pretty well convinced that only two ways exist for getting rid of the obsessive thing. One is to smash it, with either the hammer and sickle or the axe of the lictor. The other is to lift it up bodily and carry it away. Neither of these requires the activities of the magicians. One of them demands intelligence.

Faced with a panoply of unsatisfactory choices, the individual felt as powerless as the magicians higher up. Yet he could recall an idyllic past before the crash when frugal New Englander Calvin Coolidge had seen the country's chief requirement as a five-cent cigar.

"Dis gontry need five or sigs good Mussolini!"

INDIVIDUALISM

"An usher does not have to lose his identity"—Roxy

THE MONARCHIST

THE ZIONIST

THE COMMUNIST

THE FASCIST

$5,000,000,000 LIBIDO LOAN

WHAT THIS COUNTRY NEEDS IS A GOOD FIVE CENT LIBIDO

By JUNIUS, JR.

FEW of our modern scientific discoveries have received so much publicity and aroused so much immediate public interest and concern as the discovery of the libido. The business of liquidating the libido seemed to offer incommensurably greater commercial possibilities than the gas engine or the electric light. For one thing the market was limitless and the potential demand of dimensions undreamed of even by Einstein. The libido was not patented, no restriction whatever obtained. Yet what happened?

Did it develop into one of our largest industries, as well it might? Ask any school boy or girl. Or write in vain to the Department of Commerce for statistics. Even Hoover will tell you. Nothing was or could be done. Left to the mercies of rugged individualism and private initiative the scientific discovery of the libido was left practically in the laboratory stage of development. Millions of men and women still live in the pre-libido state. In a planned society such a state of affairs

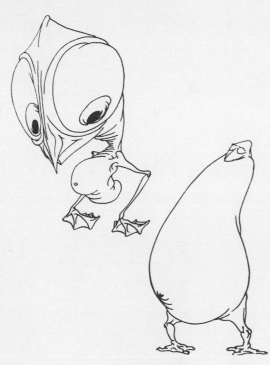

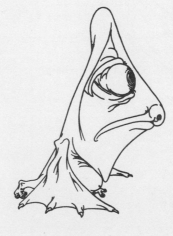

could never obtain. Here we have simply another of the contradictions inherent in capitalism; the antagonism between the private pocket and the public welfare. Only plutocrats can afford a libido, the common individual can only afford to read and dream about one. Not that a libido is so expensive to acquire, but that to all intents and purposes there is no sense acquiring it unless one is in position to use it. In fact, as matters stand, one is much worse off with a libido than without.

In place of the libido, what are we offered by the vested interests? The Republican and Democratic Parties, Seabury and Congressional investigations, Coney Island and Hollywood, Mayor Walker, Walter Winchell, Greta Garbo and the Subways, Synthetic expensive surrogates without a single calory of libido, and that is all.

Mr. Smith, the libido cannot be repealed. That goes for Hoover, Morgan and all other political and economic meddlers. You can not legislate social progress and social needs because you are not concerned with anything save perpetuating your own interests and privileges. The libido laughs at your antics. It knows what you will never learn. It has seen better and wiser and more ruthless ruling classes scrapped in the ashcan of history.

What about the liberals? Can they patch up the libido and make it serve society under the

capitalistic system? Plaster the libido how you may, it still remains a libido. Not that the liberals have failed to exert themselves. They have yawped and patched and belched. What have they achieved? Here and there an individual managed to sneak around with a libido, without falling foul of the law. But the overwhelming majority of our population are not as fortunate as the liberals, nor as well paid. Individually the liberals have snitched a divorce or two, paid alimony or blackmail, or beat it to Europe to Gourdjieff or became Zionists and Catholics—and that's about all. Socially the only reform they fostered for the socialization of the libido was Greenwich Village. And that reform proved as abortive as all their other reforms. The real estate gougers profited by it and not the masses. As was to be expected, no sooner had the libido liberalized Greenwich Village than the rents there sky-rocketed. The landlord's sole concern was and is profit not libido. And whoever hied to Greenwich Village discovered that very shortly. As the rents increased, the restaurants dimmed their lights more and more and the Villlage dissolved in the same mists as Wall Street. No one could afford a libido in the Village who could not own it in Park Ave.

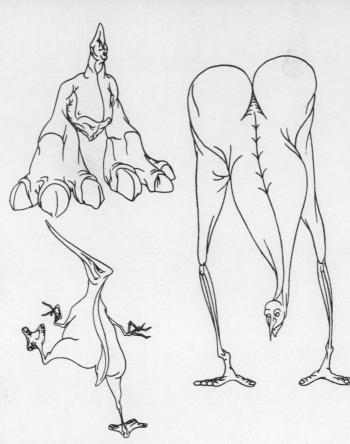

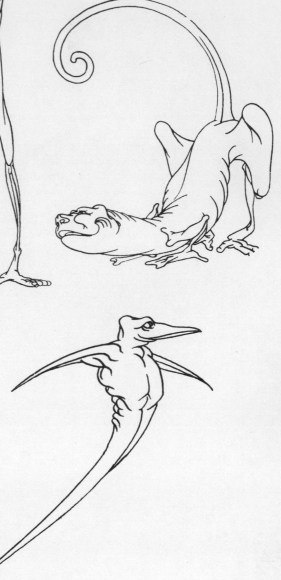

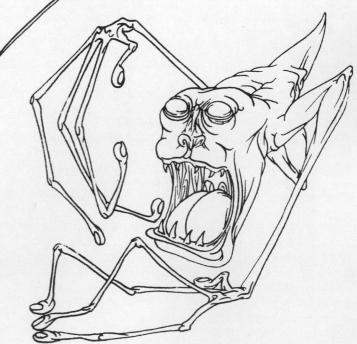

hearses for themselves. But AMERICANA will not keep quiet. It steps forward to perform its patriotic duty. Let the answer be bruited from Maine to California. Let canyons, lakes and mountains echo to a single slogan, a single purpose, a nation united. That slogan is LIBIDO; that purpose is PROSPERITY; that nation is AMERICA.

THE FIRST OF MAY

"There are signs all about us that the world is ready for a revolutionary uprising."

"Comrades, unite! You have nothing to lose but
your chains!"

"Don't talk to me about this
lousy capitalist sunset!"

"Something for The Daily Worker,
please."

ADVICE TO REVOLUTIONARIES
By LAWRENCE DENNIS

The greatest menace to communism today is the possibility of a long protracted peace during which the hardships of an ever deepening depression would stimulate the heroism of the American and British peoples to the invigoration of a moribund capitalism. At the same time the martial spirit of the nationalistic Russian communists would be sapped by a sense of comparative security from foreign attack and the vital elan of a militant communist culture would be paralyzed by the growing conservatism of a strongly entrenched bureaucracy at Moscow. As I am not an alarmist, I consider improbable an intolerably long peace; still, it is enough of a possibility to give concern to thoughtful well-wishers of communism. It goes without saying that the greater the preparations for the next war, the sooner it will begin and the greater it will be. The argument of this article is that the sooner the war starts and the more extensive it becomes, the better the chances for world communism in our time; hence good communists should hasten revolution by working for an early and disastrous war.

Instead of conducting a ludicrous campaign of democratic and bourgeois competition with the existing political parties, American communists ought to associate themselves with all movements which purport to be 100% American and which seem calculated to advance der Tag. For instance, communists should patriotically agitate for the immediate adoption of compulsory military service and for a bigger navy. The ostensible motives would be the defense of American ideals to which communists should profess devout attachment,—as a matter of gaining influence and power in the American community. The real objectives, of course, would be the training of revolutionaries for the violent overthrow of the present order and for the subsequent dictatorship of the communist minority; the preparation of American workers and farmers for the stern doctrines of communism; and, last but not least, the ultimate creation of the catastrophe indispensable for successful revolution.

Here it is pertinent to remark that while liberals and socialists talk meaninglessly about national planning, the United States Army, in a special school conducted at Washington, is training men to take over the transportation system and the key industries on the outbreak of our next war. Only our army is planning socialism. Only our next war can create the occasion for it.

Communism, like democracy, is the gift of militarism. The "oppressors" planted the first seeds of democracy and communism when, towards the end of the dark ages, they conceived the bright idea of making military use of their serfs, fiefs, vassals, colonii, slaves and villains, or when low born knaves were given the gentleman's "right to bear arms" now safeguarded by our federal constitution.

Nothing is less revolutionary than a starving, unarmed man, except two of them. To handle a hundred such wretches, one need only give ten of them food, arms and instructions to maintain law and order among the other ninety. To denounce the ten for so earning their bread or to insult the ninety for standing for it is naive and also an old communist custom.

Revolutionary leaders, ideas and grievances, real or fancied, are factors only if, when, and where the "oppressed" have been given arms by the "oppressors", not by revolutionary agitators who haven't the price of a cup of coffee. Violence without the means of effectively destroying one's adversary is insane or asinine, subject to the qualification that four legged asses are never so stupid. When a convincing exhibition of violent behavior is furnished, the strait jacket is indicated. Amateur performances, such as communist dervishes like to stage, call for firm applications of the nightstick or tear gas followed by gentle applications of iodine and cold water.

Communists should remember that if the militia of the "bosses" have shot down many a worker, the same soldiers also beheaded Charles I and butchered the whole Romanoff family in a cellar of Ekaterinbourg. Mercenaries like the Swiss guard or the members of any professional army are always more loyal to their "bosses" than a conscript army. Communists should, therefore, work for a huge standing army conscripted from the people and an adequate war crisis to infuriate such armed workers against their "bosses." Capitalists should be urged to arm and train their executioners and successors, not criticized for doing it.

Underfed, sweatshop communist fanatics, waging a curbstone competition with the Salvation Army for souls, will be no more effective against capitalism over a thousand years than revivalists have been against sin over a similar period. It is fortunate for capitalism that the British and American working classes lack military organization.

British and continental socialists have always denounced the next war and supported the present war. They are too tender, however, to exploit the military institutions or socialistic ends. Their leaders have lacked the guts of conserva-

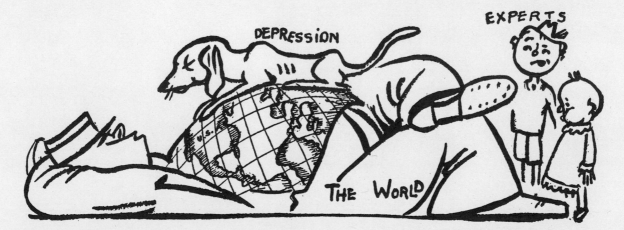

DEPRESSION

EXPERTS

THE WORLD

tives like Peter the Great, Bismarck, or Disraeli to assume responsibility for radical social changes. They have lacked the soldier qualities of a Loyola, a Bonaparte, a Mussolini, or a Lenin.

The local preachers of the British Labor Party, like Ramsey Macdonald, have long sung with Shelley, their patron saint:

> Men of England wherefore plough
> For the lords who lay ye low?
> Wherefore weave with toil and care
> The rich robes your tyrants wear.

But, when the people have taken seriously these incitements and placed such weaklings in office, the latter change their tune and sing with the same poet of the frustrated,

> I would not be a king, enough
> Of war it is to love.
> The path to power is steep and rough
> And tempests reign above
> I would not climb the imperial throne.

They lack the things that make men, not to say revolutionaries.

British and American socialism is essentially a sort of emotional masturbation practiced by impotent political agitators.

In this country our veterans have provided the only serious challenge of the depression to the established order. Everyone from President Hoover to Mr. Norman Thomas has implored the veterans not to injure public credit and business. In the face of the disapproval of the propertied classes, before which all other Americans quail, the veterans have displayed a class consciousness which is unique in our society, except among groups united by a solidarity of property interests. With little knowledge of, and less respect for, communist doctrines, the veterans have been loyal to the interests of a class which numbers in its ranks more paupers and unemployed than income tax payers or bondholders. To capitalist appeals to their patriotism, the ex-soldiers have not needed Marx to furnish the logical reply, "The rich have been getting theirs. We mean to take ours from those that have." This is the raw material of revolution;—not the constructive suggestions and offers of cooperation made to capitalism by well disposed socialists; nor yet the pathological examples of a martyr complex furnished by most of our confused communists. Revolution is the result of the will to power; not of the will to practice the golden rule or to suffer.

"Are you going to that rally to-night, Comrad?"

BALLAD OF AN INTELLECTUAL

By E. E. CUMMINGS

Listen, you morons great and small
to the tale of an intellectuall
(and if you don't profit by his career
don't ever say Hoover gave nobody beer).

'Tis Frequently stated out where he was born
that a rose is as weak as its shortest thorn:
they spit like quarters and sleep in their boots
and anyone dies when somebody shoots
and the sheriff arrives after everyone's went;
which isn't, perhaps, an environment
where you would (and I should) expect to find
overwhelming devotion to things of the mind.
But when it rains chickens we'll all catch larks
—to borrow a phrase from Karl the Marks.

As a child he was puny; shrank from noise,
hated the girls and mistrusted the boise,
didn't like whisky, learned to spell
and generally seemed to be going to hell;
so his parents, encouraged by desperation,
gave him a classical education

(and went to sleep in their boots again
out in the land where women are main).

You know the rest: a critic of note,
a serious thinker, a lyrical pote,
lectured on Art from west to east
—did sass-seyeity fall for it? Cheast!
If a dowager balked at our hero's verse
he'd knock her cold with a page from Jerse;
why, he used to say to his friends, he used
"for getting a debutante give me Prused"
and many's the heiress who's up and swooned
after one canto by Ezra Pooned
(or—to borrow a cadence from Karl the Marx—
a biting chipmunk never barx).

Or—briefly to paraphrase Karl the Marx—
'The first law of nature is, trees will be parx.' "

Now all you morons of sundry classes
(who read the Times and who buy the Masses)
if you don't profit by his career
don't ever say Hoover gave nobody beer.

This space is donated by the A. S. P. C. I.
(The Americana Society for Prevention of Cruelty to Intellectuals)

ARE YOU A LOVER of household pets?

Pedegreed Intellectuals are Ideal Home Companions!

Kinder than any other dumb animal

More Soothing than lap-dogs

Housebroken as readily and just as inexpensive in up-keep

What other Publications advertise for Sale—Americana Gives Away

A year's subscription to Americana entitles you to an A. S. P. C. I. pin and to first choice in our first carload.

For whoso conniveth at Lenin his dream
shall dine upon bayonets, isn't and seam
and a miss is as good as a mile is best
for if you're not bourgeois you're Eddie Gest
and wastelands live and waistlines die,
which I very much hope it won't happen to eye;
or as comrade Shakespeare remarked of old
All That Glisters Is Mike Gold

(but a rolling snowball gathers no sparks
—and the same holds true of Karl the Marks).

But every bathtub will have its gin
and one man's sister's another man's sin
and a hand in the bush is a stitch in time
and Aint It All A Bloody Shime
and he suffered a fate which is worse than death
and I don't allude to unpleasant breath.

Our blooming hero awoke, one day,
to find he had nothing whatever to say;
which I might interpret (just for fun)
as meaning the es of a be was dun
and I mighn't think (and you mightn't, too)
that a Five Year Plan's worth a Gay Pay Oo
and both of us might irretrievably pause
e'er believing that Stalin is Santa Clause:
which happily proves that neither of us
is really an intellectual cus.

For what did our intellectual do,
when he found himself so empty and blo?
he pondered a while and he said, said he
"It's the social system, it isn't me!
Not I am a fake, but America's phoney!
Not I am no artist, but Art's bologney!

134   Heywood Broun signing up Charlie Marx for the Socialist Follies of 1932

RED FAIRY TALES

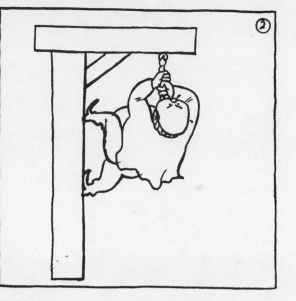

NAKED AND UNINTERESTING
By GILBERT SELDES

The Nudists have not only come to New York, but to the movies; with speaking interludes in Franco- and Teuto-English (which sound extraordinarily alike) the first picture of Nudism, *This Naked Age*, is silent. If the censor has his way, it will also be invisible. For the first time since I was press-agent for a film called Virtues. I agree with the censor.

It wouldn't be proper to bring the subject up at all, since the producers are still arguing with the New York Censors, were it not for the circumstance that the other side of the case has been pretty well canvassed and Mr. Morris Ernst has written about it in The Nation, saying, "the film was taken with delicacy, or rather in such a manner that the genitalia are never seen. Many of the snaps are beautiful. There is considerable display of buttock." Mr. Ernst is right. The psychoanalysts have a name for it.

The picture ranges from New York to France, from France to Germany, but always with one end in view, the rear end. Long shot or closeup, that is what you get. You also get a lot of exercises and the impression that when men and women foregather in nakedness, they have a deplorable tendency to do scarf-dances, without the scarves. Also they seem to dress for lunch, and eat heartily. The serious German naked-goers had little enough to eat, Heaven knows, but they seemed happy. The French ate in a chateau variously placed near Paris and in the heart of Normandy. At the dining table, you saw faces; elsewhere, the best you got was a profile. That the human being has two sets of cheeks and that one is more attractive than the other, occurred to the camera man, but he was afraid of the censor. That the male and female bodies are not identical could be judged only by an occasional far view of breasts; those of the male seemed a little less.

The snaps to which Mr. Ernst refers were beautiful when they caught scenery undefiled. The human beings who appeared, walking backward, one assumes, were not particularly pleasing in form. What they did, was exceptionally dull. It is on the ground of dullness and timorousness that I vote with the censor. The picture is as appropriate to Nudism as a skit, in Americana I think it was, all of which passed behind a screen.

At the special view, put on for a hundred or two publicists and famous people, I saw the entrance of a Great American Novelist. Great, you understand. You could even guess his name. He received, as all of us did, a slip of paper on which he was asked to give his critical opinion of the picture and to answer a lot of questions. The vital ones were: "Do you consider this picture obscene, indecent, immoral, inhuman, sacrilegious or of such a nature that it would corrupt morals, or of such a nature that it

would incite to crime?" and "Do you believe that this film should be subject to change or condemnation by any state censorship board or boards?" Natural questions. I made sure I had a pencil and sat back waiting for the picture.

But the Great American Novelist did not wait. He was hardly in his seat when he whipped out his pencil and wrote two large NO's after the questions. Then, as one having vindicated the right, he preened himself a little, and darkness descended. Choked with lack of emotion, I left the projection room the moment the picture was ended; I did not see whether the Great American Novelist changed his decisions.

It seemed to me extraordinary that the fight against the censorship is perpetually being carried on by artists, the very people who know best that a censorship is needed. They will read a manuscript and say, "It's good, but it ought to be cut." They will object to sculpture because it sprawls, to painting because it is not compact enough, to a play because it lacks concision. On the ground of art, they are all for cutting, except when the subject in hand touches on sex, when they bawl and cry like babies whose candies have been taken away. And it is not as if they were not moralists themselves. They are the first to assure you that The Decameron, being a true and full picture of life in the early Renaissance, is representative of the higher, or next year's model, morality, or that a breath of clean wild pure air blows through the Memoirs of Casanova. These, and five dozen other books, are not to be cut, although Dickens is too long and Thackeray tedious; the reason must be that morality and brevity are incompatible.

I can't bring myself quite to the point of defending the actual censors now at work in America; on the other hand, I can't bring myself to defending the work of nine out of ten artists.

As for nudism, I am unimpressed. A good love-cult, for the tabloids and the Sunday papers, I understand, wishing only that its devotees might be more lovely and a little less cultist. But nudism, as seen in the movie, seems to be a deterrent to voluptuousness —and, in fact, I have heard the argument a thousand times that for each sex to see the other always naked lessens the excitement of sex. If that is true, nudism seems to me superfluous, for the modern world supplies deterrents enough. You can read market reports or good biographies or look at newsreels or worry about the rent or grow old. There seems to be little excuse for dispensing with one of the few good inventions of our ancestors on which we have improved to the point that clothes are attractive and comfortable, merely to lower our vitality.

And if by chance the apology is a fiction, and nudism covers—if I may use the word—a profound sexual impulse, then the day of miracles is come.

OUR HEROES

HUEY P. LONG

Home-grown dictator Huey P. Long (1893–1935), known as "The Kingfish," was a senator from Louisiana, where he had been impeached in his first term as governor. He became an outspoken critic of the New Deal, proposing his own "Share the Wealth" program as he built national support for a presidential bid. Long, who maintained tight control of state politics from Washington, was assassinated during a visit to Baton Rouge.

THE SENATOR SPEAKS

By DON LANGAN

"And in conclusion, my fellow citizens, let me assure you that this is no new or idle theory of political happiness that I have come here to expound. It is just as old—and just as true—as the Scriptures themselves. Yes, I'll go back as far as you like. To Deuteronomy, to Samuel and Chronicles, to the book of Ecclesiastes. There you will find it stated almost exactly as I have stated it here today. And coming down to our own great leaders, you will find it in the speeches of that fearless Colonial liberal, Patrick Henry. You will find it in the writings of that prophet of Democracy, Thomas Jefferson. You will find it among the papers of that beloved soldier-statesman, Andrew Jackson. Indeed, my fellow citizens, you can go home and read it in the speeches of that peerless orator, Daniel Webster. We can go back into the annals of time and find example after example of the truth in my statements here today. The decline and fall of the Roman Empire, the bloody French revolution, the more recent destruction of Czarist-Russia—in the face of these, can it be denied? Do we want any such holocaust to overcome our fair land? No, my fellow citizens, a thousand times no. Let us not repeat the mistakes that have destroyed governments before us. Let us preserve this nation, with its opportunities and blessings, for the generations to come. No nation on the face of this earth, no matter how solid its foundations, no matter how extensive its resources, no matter how industrious its people, can grow in happineess and prosperity if it ignores that history-proven truth. I repeat once more: *political well-being for any people, at any time, be they part of a democracy, dictatorship or any other form of government,* lies in the fair and equal distribution of wealth. That is my mission. I thank you.

"Now look here, Snyder. I came up here today just to make a speech, and I've got to get back to Washington by morning. I can't waste any more time dickering with you like this. I told you that I could kill that proposal in committee. But, my God, man, you've got to realize that these things cost money. You could have blown me over with a light sneeze when you brought out that measly ten thousand dollars. Don't you understand that there's about four big guns to stuff in this deal besides myself? And don't get the idea that it's all smooth sailing, either. Those boys know the worth of a dollar and they can tell you goddamned quick how much noise a few thousand can make. . . . Well, all right, now you're beginning to talk sense. If the measure dies in the committee room your clients are set to save at least three quarters of a million a year, based on your business for the last three years. We can switch the levy over onto something else and let you out clean as a whistle. . . . Yes, I'll have another. Just a short one this time. . . . Well, I hadn't figured on it much but, ah, seventy-five thousand seems a plausible honorarium to my mind considering everything. . . . Why, I don't see why you say that. Where's all this business acumen you fellows are supposed to have? You do a business with the public. Raise your rates a few cents. Spread it all around. You know—equal distribution. They'll never feel it. And you'll have that money back before the Commissioners can be petitioned into forbidding the rate rise, if at all. See it? . . . Okay . . . Yes, that's preferable. Cash doesn't leave any tracks, you know. And better get down there by the end of the week. . . . Well, that's settled then. . . . Yes, you can be sure of everything. I'll see you in Washington Friday . . . Don't mention it. . . . Goodbye"

ICHTHYOLOGY

GOLD FISH

HAMILTON FISH

KING FISH

POOR FISH

BOTTOMS UP

By Irving Kolodin

With dry states as scarce as clothing salesmen in a nudist colony, it has now become merely a matter of weeks until the great drought will have passed into history, along with all the other blue laws whose aim it has been to legislate moral values. When the question of what a man should lubricate his gullet with has been taken off the nation's front pages and put back to its proper place with either the household hints or the whimsical editorial, there may be possible some perspective on the nature of this extraordinary rebellion, as expressed to date at the polls. At present, one can confidently say very that will not be mere hazard.

What one can say immediately applies largely to the externals of the affair rather than to its details; these latter, we may be sure, will remain generously opaque till the prodding finger of the researcher and historian gets around to the subject. When that moment arrives, and a final authoritative survey is compiled, there is little doubt that the primary factor in the stampede to the trough will be recognized as none other than our old friend, John Q. Depression. For, lacking the present scarcity of middle-class tax-worthy properties, one is convinced that the Eighteenth Amendment would have shambled along on its miserable course, being largely ignored, finally retiring into the shade of the Fourteenth (in the South, anyway) into that land of nullification where bad laws go when they die.

However, I need scarcely remind *Americana's* readers that times are tough for governments as well as individuals, and, since the boys that get the salaries are also the ones who pass the laws to raise the wherewithal, it was no surprise to observe that a great light suddenly appeared, and the handwriting on the wall was transformed into a mess of dollar signs. The unbelievable had come to pass. Gone were the thoughts of an "experiment, noble in purpose" . . . banished the fear that Henry Ford would shut up shop as he promised he would if the Prohibition amendment were ever repealed. What remained, only, was the thought that here, easily to hand, was a path temporarily, at least, away from the only alternative that remained . . . a way to avoid a really crushing income-tax or capital levy that would put the burden on those who could, but have not yet ever paid the bills.

Additionally, the same depression fortunately crippled the opposition; and the Anti-Saloon League has surrendered without firing a shot, save a few verbal ones. And everyone knows that elections are not won that way. Once the great oracle, John D. Jr., had not merely withdrawn his support, but plumped full-length, Movietone and all, into the other camp, as he did something more than a year ago, the jig was up. "Hamlet" without the Danish prince would be a three-ringed circus compared to the Anti-Saloon League without its Rockefeller.

Yet, in the general huzzah which is being decorously restrained until the final vote is cast, I find it difficult to join. For one thing, the bootleggers had finally achieved something like organization, and the business was running along smoothly, as the well-oiled machine it should be. For the affluent, there were the private salesman, whose fancy labels and bottles, at least, were reassuring, and whose wares were all drinkable. For the flush, there were the cordial (in plainer neighborhoods, beverage) shoppes; at least one to every residential block, and, in the more liquid sections, frequently two or three. These furnished a generally brash-tasting, but effective line of merchandise at prices that were certainly not excessive. It is a commonplace, of course, that in government controlled Canada, liquors of the level of those dispensed in the cordial shoppes are considerably more expensive, and only rarely as useable. Unless Congress shows a sagacity for which there is certainly no reasonable basis to suspect them of possessing, the same situation will shortly be upon us. Then watch the bootlegger dig in for a long stay!

For another thing, the feeble cries of personal liberty that one hears now and again have, to me, all the persuasiveness of a dollar and a quarter violin. Setting aside the fact that one's personal liberty is hedged about with many and infinitely more serious

"Come on over, we're celebratin' the return of four percent beer"

strictures than those relating merely to with what liquid one is going to accompany his indigestion, the issue comes down almost completely to personal prejudices rather than liberties.

So much for the business of liquor in the home. What the public drinking-places will come to, one can only ponder. Undoubtedly the speakeasy will be legislated out of business, and a combination drug-counter and tea-shoppe supplied to replace it. For those who can read the portents, some idea can be gleaned from the course of the beer-dispenseries.

When the 3.2 commandment was given unto the people, there arose coincidentally a clamor, probably lobbied by fixture-manufacturers on the hunt for business, that "the old-fashioned saloon must not come back." For this no one ever advanced a sizeable reason beyond intimating that somehow crime and saloons were inseparable.

Considering that organized crime enjoyed a rabbit-like fertility of development during the last decade when saloons, by statute, were universally illegal, hence non-existent, the return of the saloon might be better regarded as an omen of sobriety and order-liness. The rub, of course, is the fact that the old-fashioned saloon was the poor-man's club; his refuge from the bitter world he knew too well. Obviously no senator, representative or assemblyman is going to lobby for the poor devil who can scarcely produce a nickel for a glass of beer—not that way does re-election lie. Instead, our legislators seized upon this as the outlet for their inevitable Messianic complex and the object for all their mock-moral fervor became the saloon.

In its place, we have that weird hybrid—the Tavern-Bar-Grill-Brass Rail order of thing. Within the last six moons our larger cities and towns have witnessed a philological debauch in which anything with ten tables (or over) and a beer-tap became a Tavern, six tables, a Rathskeller, four, a Grill and anything below, either a Tap-room, a Bar or a Brass Rail. These are merely the unimaginative ones. When the fancy of the proprietor was allowed free rein, only the angels could tell what might sprout on the window-glass.

I have seen, actually, one such shop, solely dispensing beer, pretzels and free lunch solemnly labeled a "Health Farm." A few blocks away is "Ye Olde HofBrau Haus." Down the street a bit was "The Lido Rathskeller." One place effected so rapid a transformation that an awning labeled "Rector Coffee-Pot" was allowed to remain while the window blazoned "Tom's Tavern." I have searched in vain through a score of Biergarten to find so much as a potted plant, let alone a tree, while the installation of plaster-board brick fire-places and Cellutex stucco interiors has, I am reliably informed, restored the building trade to almost its 1874 level.

What will happen when the juice of the grape and the juniper berry become again lawfully obtainable, I dare not think. Let us hope, at least, that there will be no *Weinkeller* on second floors designed by God for Chop Suey parlors, and that all cafeterias be restrained, by Presidential ukase, from installing cocktail bars.

The election of 1932 was an overwhelming mandate for the Wets. The past fifteen years had proved an unworkable victory for the late-nineteenth-century temperance movement and the Prohibition Party. Since the ratification of the Eighteenth Amendment to the Constitution had prohibited manufacture, sale, and import of intoxicating liquors, bootlegging had thrived, servicing the nation's undiminished thirst. In February 1933, to the chagrin of die-hard Dries and to the glee of the beer and pretzel industries, the Twenty-first Amendment repealed Prohibition, while guaranteeing states, counties, and other administrative units the right of local option to regulate full or partial sale of alcohol. Sale of 3.2 per cent beer began in March, and in December, when Utah became the 36th state to ratify the amendment, Prohibition officially ended.

(Overleaf)
Eleanor Roosevelt (1884–1962), active in social welfare before her marriage to FDR, became in March 1933 the first president's wife to conduct her own press conference. Babies, Just Babies was a magazine Mrs. Roosevelt edited for the wealthy health-food promoter Bernarr MacFadden (the magazine had an even shorter run than Americana*).*

144   "Aw, Mithith Woosevelt, when we gonna get beer?"

NEW SOCIAL PROBLEMS

THE 3.2% DRUNK

LIQUOR CONTROL

IN MEMORIAM By E.E. CUMMINGS

A roxy is a fabulous birdy. What is a fabulous birdy? An elephancy is not a fabulous birdy.

Fabulous is not big. Fabulous is not bigger. Fabulous is not biggest. Fabulous is bigger-than-biggest.

Here is something else. You and I may ask the elephancy to perform a miracle. Any miracle will do. The elephancy looks very sad. The elephancy looks very sad because it must refuse. The elephancy must refuse because no elephancy can perform any miracle.

Now pay strict attention. You and I may not ask the roxy to perform a miracle. Only a roxyfeller may do that. When a roxyfeller asks a roxy, the roxy does not look very sad. The roxy does not look very sad because the roxy can perform any miracle which the roxyfeller asks it to perform. It is a fabulous bird. Birdies lay eggs. Ordinary birdies lay ordinary eggs.

Roxies are fabulous birdies. Roxies lay eggs.

Roxy eggs are not ordinary eggs.

Look! Here is an egg.

Is the egg an ordinary egg?—I do not think so.—Why do you not think so?—I do not think so because I never saw an egg like the egg.—Do you think the egg may be an elephancy egg?—I do not think the egg may be.—Why do you not think the egg may be?—I do not think the egg may be because I do not think that elephancies can lay eggs.—Well then, what do you think the egg may be?—A fabulous egg.

You are right: the egg is a fabulous egg.

Is the fabulous egg bigger-than-biggest?—The fabulous egg is bigger-than-biggest.—Is the bigger-than-biggest, fabulous egg miraculous?—It is miraculous. —How do you think the bigger-than-biggest, fabulous, miraculous egg came here?—I think that somebody must have laid that egg.—Who do you think must have laid it?—I do not think.—Why do you not think?—Because I know.—What do you know?—I know that roxy laid the fabulous egg.

Let us now look at roxy's egg.

It is hollow inside, like a housey. It is made of two parts. Each part is hollow. Each part is a housey. Each housey is empty. The first hollow, empty housey is the bigger-than-biggest housey of representatives and the second hollow, empty housey is the sennet. The representatives are said to lend variety to the first housey. The second housey is said to be an intimate housey because it is bigger than an elephancy's housey, which is bigger than anybody's housey, which is bigger than your housey, which is bigger than my housey, which is not founded upon a roxy.

What is now going on in both parts of the fabulous roxy egg? — Something. — Something what? — Something miraculous. — Something just miraculous? — Something miraculous and fabulous.—Something just miraculous and fabulous?—Something miraculous and fabulous and bigger-than-biggest.—What is something miraculous and fabulous and bigger-than-big-gest?—Art.—Do you think anybody makes Art? — O yes. — Who? — Artists. Are the Artists who make roxy Art bigger-than-biggest Artists?—O yes, they are the bigger-than-biggest Artists of all roxy time. — Why are the Artists who make roxy Art the bigger-than-biggest Artists of all roxy time?—Because they are K.O. —Why?—Because the acoustics are perfect.—What is an acoustic?—Damned if I know.—Why are the acoustics perfect?—Because roxyfeller asked roxy.—Do you know what the bigger-than-biggest Artists of all roxy time who make roxy Art and who are K.O. do?—O yes.—What?—Put us to sleep.—And what do we do?—Go to the powder room.—To the powder room? —Da da da.—What powder room?—Why, roxy's powder room.—Where is roxy's powder room?—O, everywhere is roxy's powder room.

Now pay strict attention.

Look around you very, very, very, carefully and tell me: what is in roxy's powder room?—I am.—Why are

"Roxy" was the nickname of Samuel L. Rothafel (1882–1936), renowned movie impresario and director of the new theatres at Rockefeller Center. Roxy was responsible for theatre names all over the country bearing the initial R of his earlier successes — the Regent, Rivoli, Rialto, and the grandest of all, the Roxy (1927). He fought bitterly to have his new theatre named for him as well, but it became the Radio City Music Hall. Opening on the rainy night of December 27, 1932, the stage show featured the synchronized dancing of 48 "Roxyettes."

The opening-night audience, which included Charlie Chaplin, Toscanini, and Amelia Earhart, discovered that one of the three cast aluminum female nudes banished by Roxy the previous week — they were too offensive for display in the theatre's elegant Bakelite and enamel decor — had nevertheless been installed on the first mezzanine. After a plea by the 24-year-old Nelson Rockefeller, William Zorach's Spirit of the Dance and Gwen Lux's Eve eventually took their places along with Robert Laurent's Goose Girl.

The censorship crisis in the RCA Building of Rockefeller Center on May Day, 1933, was not so amicably resolved. When Nelson Rockefeller asked Diego Rivera to remove the head of Lenin from his mural, the Mexican painter refused. The Rockefellers paid him his full fee of $21,000 for the unfinished wall and destroyed it the following year, despite continued protest by artists.

you in roxy's powder room?—Because I am hiding from the miraculous and fabulous and bigger-than-biggest Art of all roxy time.—And are you also hiding from roxy?—O yes.—Why?—Because I am roxy.—Who am I, then?—I guess you must be roxy, too.—You mean that we are both of us roxy?—We.

Here is something else.

What about the bigger-than-biggest Artists of all roxy time who make the bigger-than-biggest Art of all roxy time which is now going on in both fabulous parts of roxy's fabulous egg?—O, they are all roxy.—What about the fabulous gadgets for making mountains out of mole hills and what about the fabulous murals and urals and what about the goosegirl and the loosegirl and what about whathaveyou and what about everything?—O, that's all roxy.—What about the roxyfeller?—O, the roxyfeller's all roxy.—What about God? —O, He's all roxy.—God?—Didn't you know? He's the roxy of ages.

Amen.

Hark! did you hear a simply frightful noise?—O yes?—Do you think the simply frightful noise may have been a social revolution?—I do not think.—Do you think the simply frightful noise might have been a pin dropping?—I do not think.—Do you think the simply frightful noise can have been a bigger-than-biggest variety star whispering to its bigger-than-biggest variety self a hundred thousand million billion variety lightyears away?—I do not think.—Do you think the simply frightful noise could have been an intimate talking moving picture hero brushing his intimate moving talking picture teeth?—I do not think. —Speak, speak, thou fearful guest! what do you think the bigger-than-biggest, the intimater than intimatest, the absolutely fabulous and perfectly miraculous and most irrevocably immeasurable and inimitably illimitable and altogether quite inconceivably so to speak roxiest noise of all noises was?—I do not think.—Why do you not think?—Because I know.—What do you know?—I know it was Those Roxy-Bottom Blues.

"Shoe-Shine Parlor in Rockerfeller Center
(Also known as Roxy's Rancid Real Estate Romance)"

DIVERSIONS

"Oh, Mr. Considine, you always do find the coziest places."

RIVERA, STAY WAY FROM MA DOOR

By CHARLES D. YOUNG

This is written on the twenty-fifth of May and the whole mural matter at Radio Center is still undecided. Nevertheless I make the following prognosis: First of all, it will be extremely difficult for a foreign artist of no matter what distinguished talent to get commissions in this country from now on. Thanks to Diego. Second, the Rivera opus is certainly going to be covered by some native masterpiece from the taffy factory of Dean Cornwell. Third, the Rockefellers, who have for years willy-nilly purchased modern art and incidentally kept alive a few worthwhile painters, will now be encouraged to drop their culture snobbery and frankly follow their native taste by founding a Blashfield museum.

All this, thanks to Diego.

It is interesting to analyze the quarrel between the Mexican and American capitalists. Of course the Rockefellers had it coming to them since their choice of Senor Rivera was frankly dictated by their desire to cater to a prevalent craze for Mexican art, so blatantly exemplified by the muddy pseudo-vigorous picture postcards that Diego has been plastering over the innocent walls of numberless public buildings. At one stroke they were corralling the kingfish of muralists and giving the world concrete testimony of their liberal attitude, by employing a painter who had acquired fame and fortune through dramatizing the class struggle.

Rivera well deserved to collect his $21,000 and we commend him for his ability to keep intact his proletarian affiliations while subtracting such sums from the coffers of his sheepish employers. I maintain, however, that Rivera, in the role of martyr, is completely revolting, and he becomes doubly noxious by his offer to decorate gratuitously labor edifices in this country, in an attempt to nullify his crass behavior in accepting the hush money of his dupes. For there can be no doubt that the Rockefellers fulfilled their obligations hastily in order to shut him up. He rushed to the bank, pocketed the money, and at once proceeded to howl about his injured feelings. We are wasting no sympathy on the Rockefellers to whom $21,000 is a mere bagatelle, but we are unable to rouse ourselves into any sort of frenzy about the injustice that Rivera suffered when we take cognizance of the fact that his artist employees received a weekly salary of thirty dollars or less.

But certainly all this would be forgiven and forgotten, and one might even be tempted, out of an instinctive allegiance for the craftsman against the capitalist, to take sides on behalf of the Mexican painter, if one could call to mind one single instance in the whole life of the man that was distinguished by a gracious, disinterested motive. Remember that even in the days when the public buildings of Mexico were turned over to her artists for the delineation of the upward struggle of the Mexican masses, and painters like Orozco received masons' wages, good old Diego managed to wangle himself a good fat salary as a sort of supervisor of the works.

The Rockefellers would have been wise if they had learned from the artists, who esteem Mr. Rivera but little, from true proletarian sympathizers, who have learned to give him a wide berth, and from his talented Mexican compatriots, who have for years viewed his antics with supreme, if unpublicized, disdain.

TECHNOCRACY

A Yacht for Every Home

At Christmas time in the dreary winter of 1932, the nation's press exploded with news, analysis, and furious debate on the subject of Technocracy. A letter to the New York Times traced the coinage of the word to a 1919 pamphlet by a Berkeley engineer, but in its current usage Technocracy was the brainchild of Howard Scott (1890–1970) and stood for his opinion, derived from Thorstein Veblen, that the introduction of the machine into modern industry, with the resulting unemployment, meant the end of the price system as we know it. Technocracy would introduce a new currency based on units of energy.

Over six feet tall, Scott was an evasive, yet charismatic figure, a former Village character said to have written articles for the IWW. For the past twelve years, he had directed a research group at work on the implications of his theory. In 1932 he headed the Energy Survey of North America under the auspices of Columbia University. As spokesman for the research group, Scott caught the attention of the press, which built Technocracy into a national furore by provoking and recording angry rebuttals by industrialists, scientists, and churchmen. Scott published an article in the January 1933 Harper's, soon issued in book form. Responses ran from Communists William Z. Foster and Earl Browder's pamphlet reporting the Soviet view to a Collier's article, "Technocracy Made Simple." The March issue of Judge was devoted to a spoof, with a cover drawing by Dr. Seuss (see p. 13). By that time, however, the craze was over. On January 24 front-page headlines had announced that his Columbia colleagues had sacked Scott and disbanded his group. Scott went into temporary seclusion while reporters searched vainly for his college and employment records, and the country had to await the solutions of the New Deal and, eventually, of John Maynard Keynes. Undaunted, Scott himself reemerged the following year as leader of a national Technocracy movement, and his followers to this day wear its symbol, the chromium and vermillion monad, a sign of balance.

152   THE BIG GUNS ANNOUNCE THAT THE DEPRESSION IS MERELY A STATE OF MIND

TO HELL WITH WORK
By AUSTEN H. ROBINSON

Based on the assumption that America enjoys a providentially unique geographic position, and is a potentially self-sustaining economic unit, Technocracy proposes a government by scientific experts. It is maintained, that our high state of technological achievement makes the price system an anachronism, since it is possible with little effort to produce an overabundance of the physical requirements of life. Technocracy, through its spokesman Mr. Howard Scott, suggests that we substitute energy determinants, actual and potential, such as coal, water-power, chemicals and human ingenuity, for our worthless and obsolete system of credits and currency.

"The Machine has now made possible and necessary, the elimination of much of man's toil. It has rendered political systems useless. It has sounded the death-knell of old methods of exchange. It has shelved permanently the necessity for private enterprise and savings" . . . Wayne W. Parrish.

This statement comes not from pen of a Marxian idealist or muddle-head, it is printed in Mr. Al Smith's magazine and was written by an able elucidator of Technocracy.

How come?

We'll explain it to you.

Remember we are a nation of scientists. Every American housewife who uses an electric iron or vacuum cleaner considers herself something of an engineer. The American male is the world's most notorious tinkerer and the mere ownership of a flivver makes him an expert on internal combustion engines.

Hence, any revival meeting run by science is sure to pack 'em in. Technocracy makes no really unbelievable claims excepting of course its assertions regarding the high scientific standing of its patron saint Mr. Howard Scott.

But that is a minor matter.

Mr. Scott, as the master of ceremonies of this scientific floor-show sponsors the following statement: "With what is known of technology today in this country, it is now necessary for the adult population to work but 660 hours per year per individual to produce a standard of living ten times above the average income of 1929."

This sounds more than agreeable as does the proposition that we are to abolish the price system.

In fact we wholeheartedly endorse his notion of installing unbreakable electric bulbs, everlasting razor-blades and washable toilet-tissue. We have always suspected the manufacturers were giving us a lousy break.

The one thing that puzzles us just the least little bit, is, how Mr. Scott and his scientific cohorts expect to put this deal across. Are the boys who have all the marbles now going to cough up their plunder, relinquish their power, and put a bunch of unemployed experts from Columbia University in charge?

And if they won't, what's the use of telling us with so much statistical detail what swell times we might be having? We know damned well that the dignity of labor has been much exaggerated. There is no glory and little prestige in sweeping a public thoroughfare during a sixty mile gale.

In short, has anybody among the Technocrats developed a technique for throwing out the present inefficient incumbents of power? Or will they be retired on a pension of ten million Energy Determinants per year?

But, we suppose, these unimportant details will be dealt with shortly. In the meantime we beg to point out that eminent economists have written ably and exhaustively on the subject of Technocracy without arousing the slightest ripple of interest outside their specialized circles. It required the inspired touch of the publicity man to make these dull matters into conversational small change for the hoi polloi.

Scott, who has been credited by Technocrats with amazing engineering feats, has disavowed most of these claims when they were checked up or challenged. He has proven an amiable enough dictator for the time being and has nothing to fear from the State Department, despite his extremely revolutionary notions.

We have always cherished scientific quacks in this great country of ours and it is perhaps the humane intention of the Technocrats to divert our much harassed minds momentarily at least from our real troubles. Our wealthy fellow citizens are frankly terrified, and —anxious to remain in possession of their Lalique bathtubs and fake Rembrandts—they avidly listen to the pseudo-scientific gurglings of maestro Scott. Their interest is due to a complete misunderstanding of the meaning of Technocracy. They would be horrified to discover that somewhere someone is preparing a huge vacuum cleaner equipped with tornado-like powers of suction, which is likely to sweep all of them into the sanitary garbage can of the future.

MECHANICS

"The Machine has freed Man for Higher Tasks"

"The Machine has freed Man for Higher Tasks"

MODERN FAIRY TALES

THE DIGNITY OF LABOR

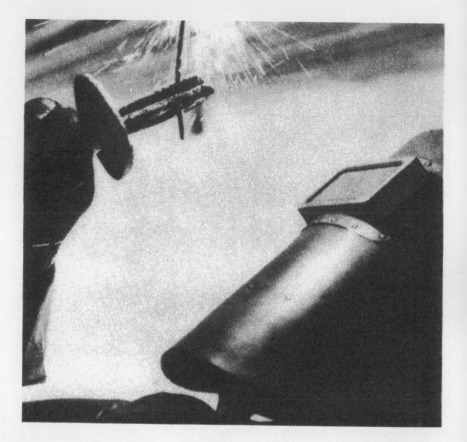

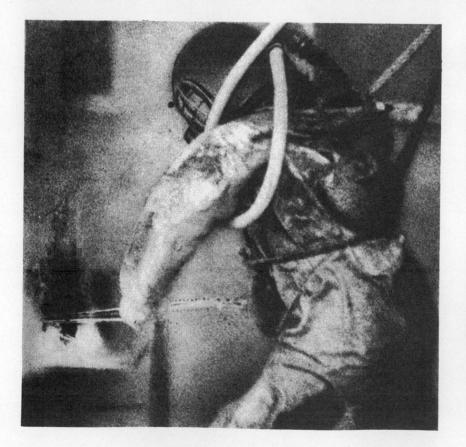

SECRETS OF INDUSTRY

How Flounders are made

UNOFFICIAL OLYMPICS

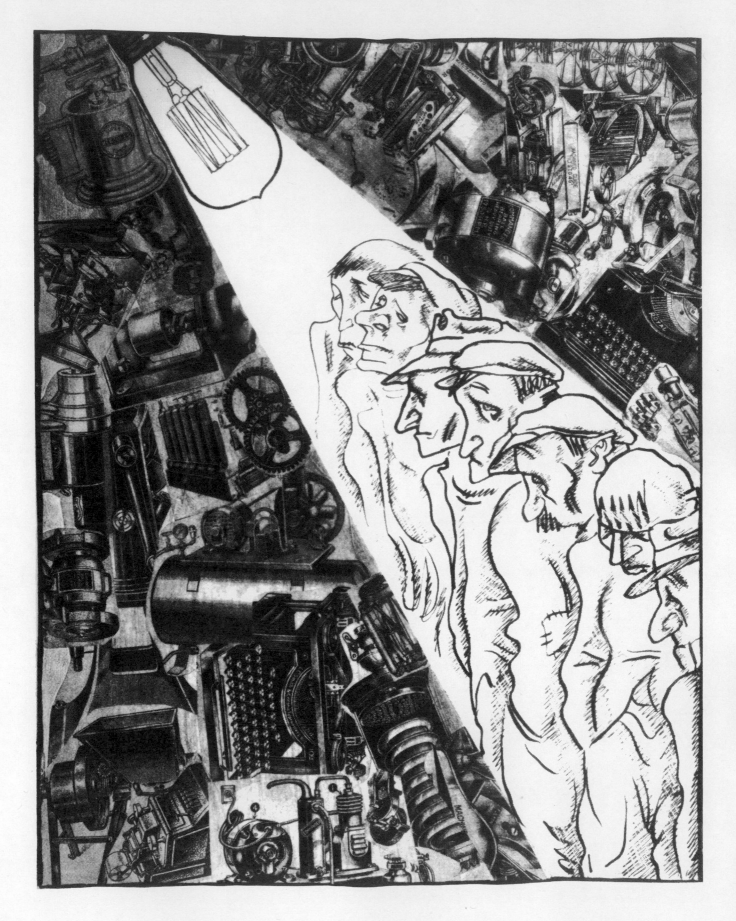

AMERICA WINS AGAIN: Greatest number of unemployed in the whole civilized world

IN MEMORIAM: TECHNOCRACY

"Imagine, we'll only have to work four hours a week!"

IMMIGRATION

"You go back where you came from, Mr. Einstein; we got plenty of unemployed astrologers of our own."

Physicist Albert Einstein (1879–1955) accepted an appointment to the Princeton Institute for Advanced Studies in October 1932. He visited California briefly that winter, then returned to the Continent. A few months later the Nazis confiscated his property in Germany, forcing his family to join him in exile. He sailed for the United States in October 1933 to take up his appointment at Princeton, where he remained until the end of World War II.

THE DECAY OF ANTI-SEMITISM

By JUNIUS, Jr.

To keep the Jews as a going concern, it has been found necessary for thousands of years to bolster up this unstable people by Anti-Semitism.

That they survived at all is unfortunate. It was primarily due to the primitive state of technology at the time of their historical emergence. Birth Control was not then at hand for disposing of them wholesale and on the spot. So there were the Jews left to be dealt with. But how?

What more than suffices to qualify other candidates for society could never suffice for the Jew. Happily our progenitors recognized from the first that it was a waste of time to knock out his front teeth or to subject the Jew to other simple and humane ceremonies of initiation. Circumcision might do for purposes of identification. But methods obviously gruelling were in order for the gruesome task of forcing the Jews to function within the framework of society without at the same time universally undermining its very foundations, confidence and credit. Anti-Semitism is, was, and will be the only discipline that can humanly be devised to nullify the congenital incompatibility and the disruptive influence of the Jew. More than an antidote, it, and it alone, can provide sufficient collateral upon which the Jews may be extended limitless credit. Moreover not only does it turn the Jew into an acceptable credit-risk but it is the only way of compelling the Jews to accept, tolerate and extend anything to or for each other.

Naturally, the task of sustaining anti-Semitism, and thus human society, and incidentally the Jews, engrossed the outstanding minds of every generation. In fact, it grew into an esoteric cult. Anti-Semitism thrived and so did the Jews.

But, now, at the time when our international credit structure is critically impaired, we find that anti-Semitism is on the verge of bankruptcy. Small wonder, how could it survive, if we entrust, as we have, the task of maintaining it to realtors, or exclusive societies, hysterical even if farsighted Ku Kluxers, themselves Jews, and such gentile subalterns as Chesterton, Ford, or Hitler (not a Brisbane among them). In the good old days, these hacks would have been at best assigned to supervise only such minor details as maiming, raping or extirpating a few score Jewish paupers,—in order to impress upon the public how futile are these extemporaneous methods of maintaining credit stability.

Observe the world. The anti-Semitic Who's Who reads like a subscription list to an asylum for the feeble minded. Where do we find anti-Semitism organized, even if abortively, on a national scale? Poland, Germany, Roumania, Austria . . . . but why continue? All are third or fourth rate countries, or nations so disrupted as to be hopelessly ineffectual. Those nations which are foremost at present, and which in the past have always assumed the leading role, all are to-day dragging hopelessly at the tail-end. In the U.S.A. as well as abroad everything is left to the whim of personal initiative. Here and there, a Minister in the doldrums, or an executive bored with antiques raises a halting alarm; and as much of his appeal as can be heard over the protests of advertisers is immediately snatched up and vulgarized by any number of professors, clerks, shopkeepers and editors. Men who would have never dared to do more than swing a club or toss a faggot, now theorize openly on the subtleties of anti-Semitism. Worst of all are, of course, the Jews themselves who are selfishly anxious for publicity and hence shriek about over-emphasis. The virulent obsession is abroad that anti-Semitism is a layman's privilege.

To those who are entrusted with the destinies of our nation and of the world, we issue this warning. The most destructive trait in mankind is its proclivity to make a virtue out of necessity. Societies function normally only so long as the fraud underlying them is fully recognized, efficiently screened and adequately exploited; otherwise they invariably crash. The Jews will remain with us. Our technical advances are still too limited to enable us to cope with them otherwise than in the past. Besides, now is no time for experiment. Society must be made safe for anti-Semitism.

"Oh, one of the Kentucky Horowitzes!"

"You endorse this hair tonic, Mr. Einstein, and we'll put you across in a big way!"

PROBLEM IN PHYSICS

Einstein takes a hair-cut

CHICAGO WELCOMES YOU

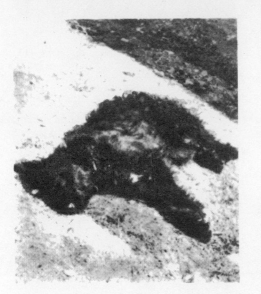

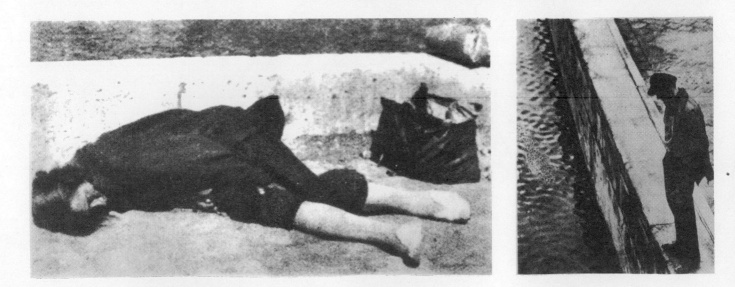

The Chicago World's Fair of 1933, entitled "A Century of Progress,"
attracted hundreds of thousands of visitors during the summer and fall.

SOME FACTS
OF LIFE

"Me old lady says dat no decent girl needs to wash herself so much."

"Gee, nature's swell ain't it?" "Yeh, 'specially when its happens outdoors."

SAY IT WITH FLOWERS

CHILDHOOD

ADOLESCENCE

MATURITY

INHIBITION

MIDDLE-AGE

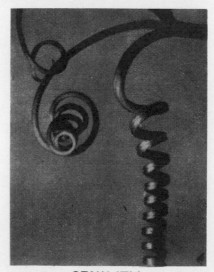

SENILITY

THE FACTS OF LIFE

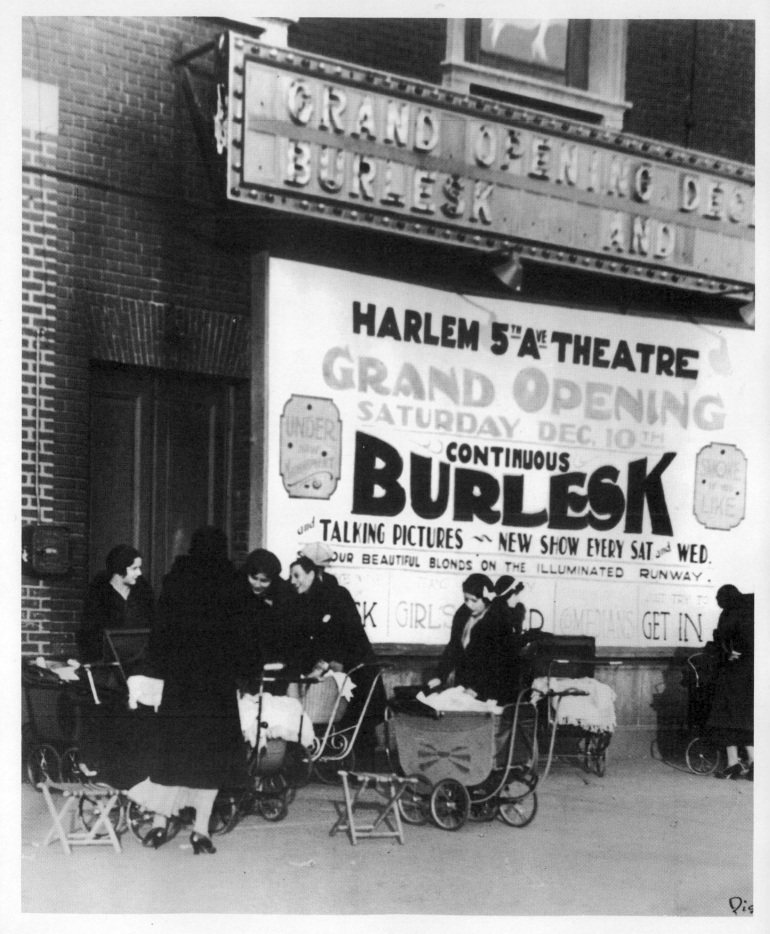

Well, one thing leads to another . . . .

THE AMERICANA
PRIZE-WINNER

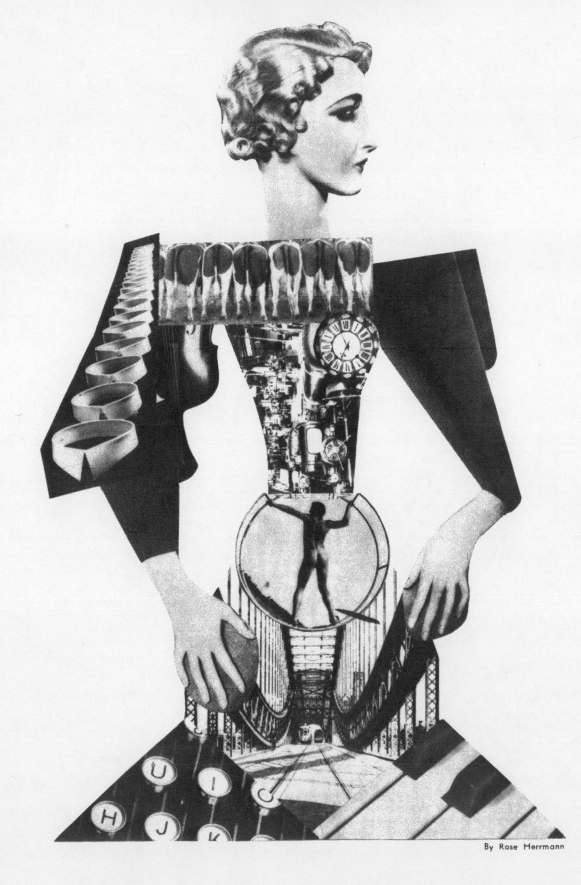

By Rose Herrmann

THE ALL-AMERICAN GIRL

THE WILL TO POWER

DECORATION

"THE LEGITIMATE AND ILLEGITIMATE STORK"
Proposed mural for a maternity home

HOW IT BEGAN

SOCIETY FOR THE PREVENTION OF VICE

SWELLS

"This is our last night together, until I return from my honeymoon."

SOCIETY

"I must come to see you play polo."

SOCIETY

Socialite Donald D. Drone, with that sparkling
divorcee, Mrs. Rita P. Bubble

The Dowager Mrs. M. Miller Tassle-Swagger

Mr. Chanticleer Q. Clucker of Newport

Miss Pauline Percher Pointlass, in conversation
with Bobby de Bouncer

"Say, old man, I've got a feeling that one of us is an anthropologist."

EXPLORATION

Mrs. Martin Johnson returns with a few pets.

"What a beautiful day! Let's
go out and kill something!"

"We must hire some new servants; I've
borrowed the cook's last dollar."

Addition

His Ancestors came over on the Mayflower

"Of course we could live cheaper in France but we can only get credit in America."

Subtraction

"Larry, leave the room! I have something to say to papa."

"Fancy meeting you here! Well, well, it's a small world after all!"

NEW YORK: PLAYGROUND OF THE NATION

W ITH ITS TWO NEW architectural wonders, the Empire State Building (1931) and Rockefeller Center (1931–39), New York was poised at the edge of an uneasy continent, about to receive the refugees of an uneasy world into its stone heart. Center of the fashion and garment industry, of theatre and broadcasting, home of the nation's most influential magazines and publishing firms, and financial capital of the world, the city now had Hoovervilles spreading in the parks at its feet.

"This little proposition is only interesting to executives."

"Good morning, this is the Municipal Morgue — whom did you wish to speak to?"

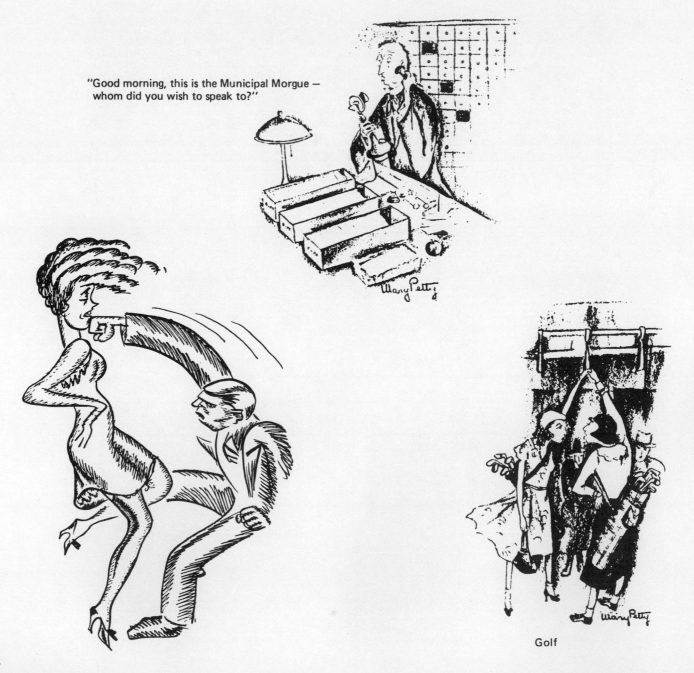

Golf

184

THE SIDEWALKS OF NEW YORK

BUY AMERICAN

AS ADVERTISED

IS THIS ASTRONOMY?

SOCIOLOGY

By George Grosz

THE NEW LEISURE CLASS

IN DARKEST HARLEM

"Mr. Livingston, I believe!"

Americana cover, February 1932

A strong and self-contained business and residential center of upper Manhattan, Harlem became the largest black community of America in the early decades of this century. Black poets and writers, nurtured by the Harlem Renaissance of the 1920s, guided white intellectuals into the vibrant culture north of 125th Street. *Americana* not only mocked their somewhat self-conscious forays into an alien territory, but conveyed an appreciation of the formal beauty in this exotic urban scene. The famous Harlem rent parties offered a vivid contrast to the breadlines, and many *Americana* artists drew them both.

Hard hit by the Depression, Harlem was still described by artists of the period as the most stimulating environment outside of Paris. And to any white New Yorker with the means to head uptown, it meant music, dancing, and fun. When the prominent Berlin art historian and print curator Curt Glaser visited New York in 1932, *Americana* contributor Adolf Dehn took him to Harlem. Glaser, who would be dismissed by the Nazis the following year, called the Savoy Ballroom the high point of his trip to America. The Savoy was packed every night, even before Benny Goodman immortalized its Stomp. Miguel Covarrubias had recorded the Stomp, the Lindy Hop and other principal dance steps of Jazz Age Harlem in his *Negro Drawings* of 1927, at-

tracting other caricaturists to Harlem subjects. Al Hirschfeld included a scene in a Harlem bar in his brilliant tour of speakeasies, *Manhattan Oases* of 1932.

Although we laugh at the *Americana* artists' savage dealings with the faces of Hoover and Roosevelt, their treatment of anonymous Harlem figures is often disquieting. Whether in Europe or America, few comic publications of the time were free of the stereotypical treatment of blacks that had been a prominent sidestream of American graphic humor throughout its history. In the cartoons of the German *Simplicissimus* or Hergé's *Tintin* in Belgium, in America's daily newspapers or its long-lived comical magazine *Judge* (where a fine black cartoonist E. Simms Campbell found a market), exaggerated black faces were thought to be funny. This tendency was deepened, perhaps, by twentieth-century artists' study of African masks. A serious interest would sometimes inform an ordinary drawing with distortions of a peculiar, almost anthropological, intensity. Other so-called ethnic humor in this and other magazines has little redeeming quality. While no one asked an *Americana* cartoon to resemble an *Opportunity* cover, some of the art deserves the disfavor with which we, our vision partially corrected since the 1960s, now regard it.

191

"I'm so grateful to you for bringing me,

simply adore the natives!''

L. v. Beethoven's
"Sixth Symphony"
(Pastorale.)

Awakening of joyful feelings on arrival in the country.
Erwachen heiterer Empfindungen bei der Ankunft auf dem Lande.
Allegro ma non troppo. (♩=66)

King

"Yeah Man!"

ALL GOD'S CHILLUN GOT FUN
By IRVING KOLODIN

With the rest of the world arrayed on its collective backsides, legs kicking with the futility of so many inverted beetles, it is comforting to note that at least one segment of the populace retains its capacity for laughter, genuine and unabashed. The reference, obviously, is to the negro. Having had nothing, he has lost nothing. He is, perhaps, sickened by the heavings of the Ship of State; but he has the solace, at least, of honestly cursing the captain, divorced from the politeness of blood-brotherhood. He works (if he can), he brawls, above all, he plays . . . richly, fully, madly, shaking with a joy that reduces us to envious silence.

Some night when you have endured the gilded banalities of a Broadway music show, drop your program into the nearest ashcan and take yourself to a midnight performance at the Lafayette Theatre, up where Seventh Avenue has green grass and benches down its middle. Any one of their nights is likely to be good, but if you want to observe the festivities at their giddiest, wait for Maestro Chick Webb and his orchestra, but more particularly watch for an occasion when the unapproached, unapproachable Louis Armstrong is socking it out, when this latter-day Angel Gabriel is gathering his flock unto him.

Aside from the pure connoisseurs of his art, the house is sprinkled with musicians, even more white ones than black, a modernist composer or two . . . all out to pick up a few new licks from the greatest of them all. A blast from the Webb outfit, on the stage, and from the wings trots out a little brown man, gleaming like a new pair of shoes, in a tuxedo and a turn down collar, his face slit with a grin, dangling a handkerchief from his left hand, and from his right, a sleek, fabulously glittering trumpet. The applause, of course, is earshattering . . . palms smash together, feet stamp, lungs pour forth shrill whistling . . . are they glad to see him. No claque here! It's all on the level . . . this audience knows what's coming. He sidles up to microphone on the stage, and from a cluster of horns overhead, a froggy voice issues. What has gone into that belly to make those vocal chords what they are, one can only imagine. And he stutters a little, too. But you gather that the first number will be an old favorite . . . "Ain't Misbehavin'." Armstrong fancies himself a vocalist and, leaning over the mike, he intones the first chorus. The tune eludes him, but what he does with the words and rhythm is audible joy. He surrounds the astonished microphone with his arms, pleading, cajoling, leering at it, pouring out the anthem in a voice that would melt an iceberg . . when he doesn't like the words, he slides off into a guttural mouthing of syllables that

is irresistible. Then he raises the trumpet to his lips and goes to town. Name your own odds to wager that the composer himself could identify the tune, with Armstrong embellishing it with comments, footnotes and variations that are ingenuity gone insane. A tone of burnished brilliance, a rhythmic sense infinitely insinuating, descending and ascending *portamenti* that are absolutely a unique talent, high-flung Ds, Es, and a final preposterous F that is simply not in the instrument. Richard Strauss prepares, in his scores, any high C with at least three notes to get the trumpeter up there, but Armstrong pops out *ten* of these successively before exploding an ecstatic F that leaves him tottering around the stage while his audience raises a hysterical clamor for more.

He announces "When You're Smiling" and this time he has a new act. He backs off, downstate left, leans half-way over like a quarter-miler, begins to count, (swaying as he does) "one, two, three". . . he has already started racing toward the rear where the orchestra is ranged, and as he hits four, executes a slide and a pirouette; winds up facing his audience and blowing the first note as the orchestra swings into the tune. It's mad, it's meaningless, it's hokum of the first order, but the effect is electrifying. No shabby pretenses about this boy! He knows what his audience will take to their hearts, and how he gives it to them. His trumpeting virtuosity is endless . . . triplets, chromatic, accented, eerie counterpoints that turn the tune inside out, wild sorties into the giddy stratosphere where his tone sounds like a dozen flutes in unison, all executed with impeccable style and finish, exploits that make his contemporaries sound like so many Salvation Army cornetists. Alternately singing, choruses and daubing with the handkerchief at throat, face, forehead (he perspires like a dying gladiator) the while a diamond bracelet twinkles from his wrist, he finally gets off the stage to rest.

But within an hour he is back again, playing (as he says "for the musicians in the house") fourteen choruses of that famous *passacaglia* "Tiger Rag", "Limehouse Blues", "Sleepytime Down South", blowing, daubing, singing, blowing, with incredible energy, till his breath is absolutely gone and his exhausted audience straggles out into the starlight, chattering about a boy with a horn.

Well, don't say that *Americana* didn't tip you off . . . the local authorities inform us that a dead-line for Carl Van Vechten has been established at 125th Street, with orders to shoot on sight if he is discovered in the tenderloin . . . Armstrong is back, and the Lafayette is trembling these nights with life and laughter . . .

195

IS THIS CULTURE?

America's greatest contribution to World Civilization

THE GAY WHITE WAY

YOUR BROADWAY AND MINE

RESIGNED TO LIVING
By EMANUEL EISENBERG

(A play about three people who disliked each other very much)

The curtain rises on an apartment which is a composite of wealthy-bohemian styles in decoration in Paris, London and New York. Noel Coward (Xmas Coward? Xmas Card? Oh, all right, let's drop it) is discovered on a couch in a state of high irritation. Near him, on a divan, is Lynn Lunt equally exacerbated; and at the other end of the room, in an easy chair, is Alfred Fontanne, so furious that there is no containing himself.

LYNN (lighting a cigarette). But, my dear Noel, do you realize that all your comedies are about the same thing? The uproarious joke in every one of them is the eternal and hopeless squabble between people with a sense of obligation to society and those with a supposedly delicious irresponsibility

The home life of the Lunts as Aunt Sarah imagines it to be.

NOEL (taking some brandy). Well, you've been turning in the same performance for God knows how many years now.

ALFRED (taking some sherry). I fail utterly to see what possible connection that has with it.

NOEL (lighting a cigarette). Only the connection of a continuity in abuse, if continuity has any more dramatic validity . . . and if abuse is to become the final substance of high comedy.

ALFRED. Whatever it is, you're talking of the lady I've been meaning to make my wife for a very, very long time.

LYNN (fixing herself a whisky and soda). Well, as I was saying when I was so shrewdly interrupted—

NOEL. You weren't interrupted at all, my dear. You were supplemented.

LYNN. Supplemented! That sounds horrible. As if I were a serial in a daily paper that had to run for weeks and weeks yet.

ALFRED (lighting a cigarette, since he is the only one so far who hasn't done so). Maybe we're all unfinished serials. Only—our lives scarcely rise to a dramatic climax every day, do they? How should you like the last paragraph of today's installment of you to read, my dear, my very dear Lynn? Somehow I am unable to vision that skirt of yours supporting you cosily from the edge of a precipice.

NOEL (putting out his cigarette, lighting a new one, finishing his brandy and pouring himself some sherry, all at once). Would you all mind very, very much if I changed a line at this point? After all, it's my play and it's my privilege to think that something much funnier could be said right now than the line we've been using.

LYNN. Is it going to be something riotously comic that is sure to start an interminable quarrel?

ALFRED. And will no one be in character any more, which is the case in all your plays when the theme is abandoned, my dear, naughty, very clever Noel?

NOEL. Now *that* I resent.

ALFRED. Noel Coward Resents a new play by himself called Design For Private Living.

NOEL. That wasn't worthy of you, Alfred.

ALFRED. Not worthy of *you*, Noel, my boy. You wrote it. I'm saying *your* lines, I am.

LYNN. How about getting back to the subject, you gay lads? You may not remember it, and the audience may not, either—but I'm moving in one direction, and I mean to get there, willy nilly.

NOEL (exploding). Willy nilly!

ALFRED (joining). How about higgledy-piggledy?

LYNN (beginning to titter). Lovely, lovely.

NOEL. And wishy-washy. I *adore* wishy-washy.

They all begin to roll over the apartment in paroxysms of delight. This goes on for fifteen minutes or so.

LYNN (suddenly sitting up tensely). Noel, you've got to take me seriously. I can't bear this much longer. You must tell me: are you interested in the comedy of character? or in the comedy of situation with almost no reference to the particular people involved? Don't you care *how* they got involved? or how, once they're in it, their reactions differ from the reactions of any others who might get similarly complicated?

NOEL. You remind me of a Mr. Trogswell I met in Bombay.

ALFRED. You mean that fellow with the double goitre who insisted on wearing stiff collars during the day?

NOEL. The very one. Shall I tell you about Mr. Throgswell?

LYNN. I just can't wait to find out.

NOEL. Mr. Throgswell had a theory about emotions and their relation to the vowel sounds of language. Suppose you were French and someone said "cocu". What would your response be? Sheer amusement. The muscles of the mouth and jaw produce a sensation of casual pleasure in this physical performance, and the consequent emotion is amiable indifference. But say it in English. Say "cuckold". What happens? Suspicion and frenzy. The click of the tongue against the roof creates a dull, hollow sound; the short vowels bring one up stiffly; misery follows very, very soon. . . . I hope I make myself quite clear?

ALFRED. You haven't told her what finally happened to Mr. Throgswell.

NOEL. Mr. Throgswell departed this world after an attack of bile, induced by the slow pronunciation of "cellar door", which he was informed had been chosen by a foreign lady as the most beautiful sounds in our speech.

LYNN (rising grimly to light a brandy and mix herself a cigarette). I suppose this is going to continue indefinitely, this business of beginning with a perfectly sober and valid theme, of which nothing sound is ever made, and proceeding charmingly to nonsense which is fairly diverting nonsense but which never has any real growth out of the situation and rarely seems credible as coming from the particular characters?

NOEL. Oh, yes. Very, very indefinitely.

ALFRED. It's been going on this way for years. Don't you know about Noel? He's one of those versatile boys. Versatile, that's what he is. "Hay Fever" and "Private Lives" and "Design for Living" on the one hand, and "The Vortex" and "Calvacade" on the other. A marriage of viewing-with-alarm and what-the-hell's-the-difference.

NOEL. You just wait. Some day I'm going to write a play that isn't tenuous and isn't brittle and not even highly polished—and then you'll be sorry for everything you've said.

ALL. Tenuous! I love tenuous! Brittle! Brittle kills me. Highly polished! I adore highly polished.

Holding their cigarettes low and their drinks high, they collapse with laughter. The curtain, seeing them unaware, hurriedly sneaks down.

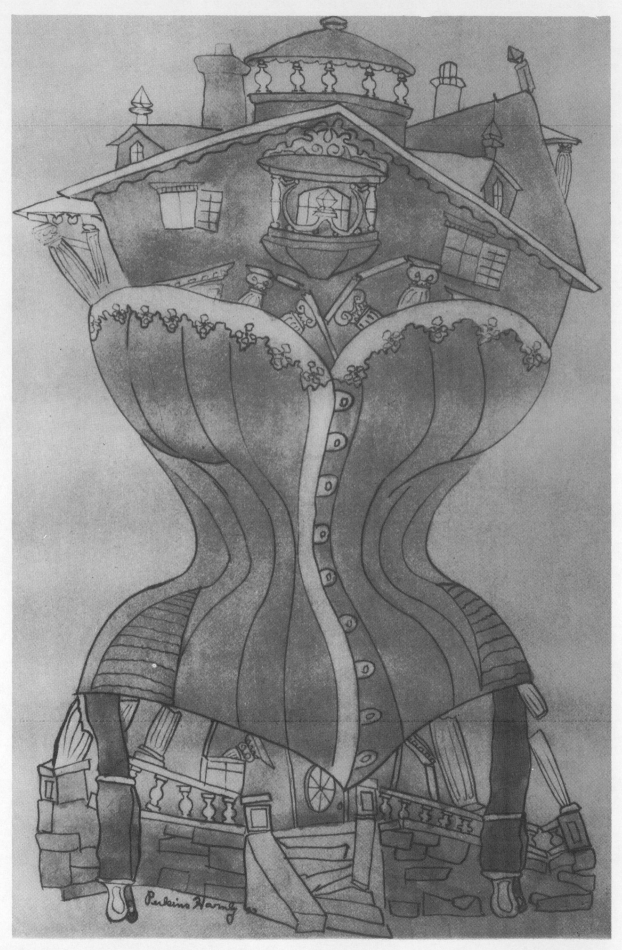

THE MAE WEST INFLUENCE

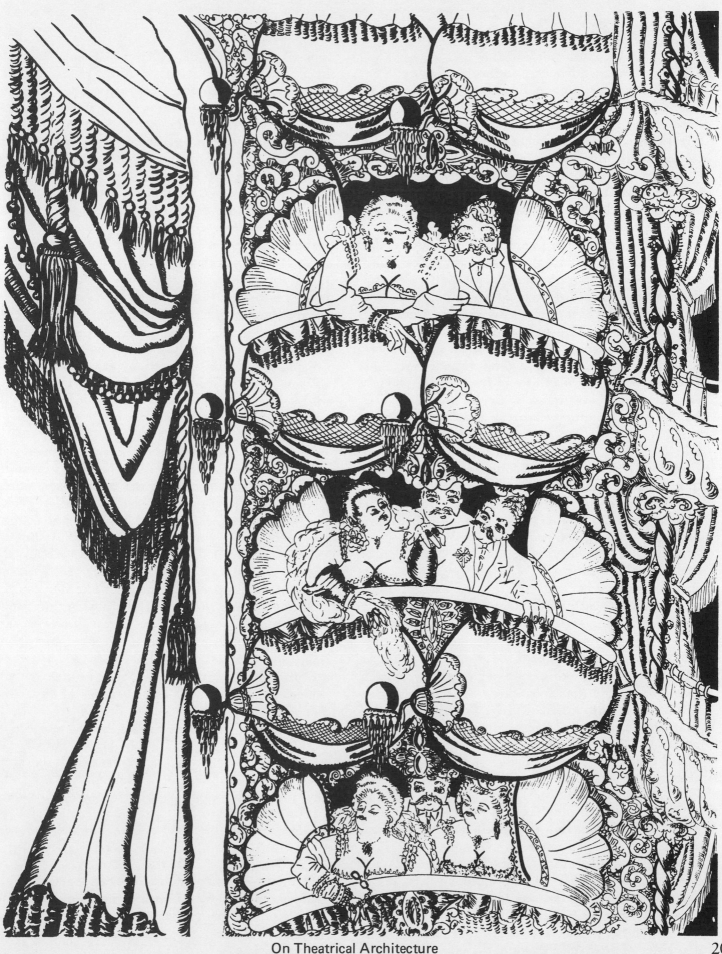

On Theatrical Architecture

THE THEATRE

By B. G. GUERNEY

The gala 75,000th performance is a stupendous tribute to that sombre and fantastic allegory, *The Flea Circus*. Its run on Broadway has been surpassed by no other play, not excepting *Abie's Irish Rose*. The Spring of 1925 saw the opening performance, and twelve generations of actors have earned their blood in this masterful production. It might be little short of presumption, therefore, to point out at this late date the poignant universality of this drama, for, as one of the minor characters murmurs in the sun-parlor of the Flea's Hotel (a remarkably fine bit of acting, by the way): "What's it all about, anyway, Rudolph? Eh? . . . A few hours of care-free childhood,—and then we're clapped into a house with deceptive glass-walls; we butt our heads against them, till our hearts break, and we are deprived of our god-sent gift of spurning the earth, of leaping heavenward . . . Next, the chain-gang of marriage . . . Then the exhibitionism of our frail, futile talents: you, Rudolph, pushing a merry-go round several hundred times your weight; I dancing in a scaramouche's frock! . . . What for, Rudolph? Tell me! . . . Why, just for our daily blood! . . . Love, Rudolph? Come, now, you ought to be the last one to talk about that! What *does* our sex life amount to, Rudolph? A piquant suctorial proboscis, a trim waist, a half a dozen slim ankles,—and you're caught, Rudolph, you're *caught!* . . Why, we can't even pass our hardily won accomplishments on to our immediate progeny! Look at me, now: I can juggle a ball, using only two of my legs, the same as the Japs; I can push a steamroller, and do a jig and even recite,—but do you think my little Mortimer will be able to carry a flag, even? . . . No, Rudolph! . . . And what if we do at last attain to the ripe and honored old age of twoscore and ten days? Why, the Master rewards us with a Golden Collar, and puts a magnifying glass before us, so that we may find childish entertainment in the antics of the odd, miscroscopic creatures whose blood we drink! Life,—Love,—Glory,—Power,—they're just a lot of Flit, Rudolph, just a lot of Flit! . . . *Ekkh*, Rudolph, but I am a-weary! . . ."

The plot of the play is an old Byzantine legend, which has filtered into the folklore of all nations. It formed the substance for innumerable plays, paintings and pageants. Holbein's *Dance of Death*, Reinhardt's *Miracle*, and in more modern times, Noel Coward's *Vortex*, are definitely indebted to this imperishable and anonymous masterpiece.

It is the story of Flearette, the gay, the capricious daughter of a travelling mountebank, whose beauty imperils the heart of a prince. As presented in Prof. Heckler's performance, a high point of drama is achieved in the interview between the ruling monarch and his love-lorn son. "Remember," says the aged father, "the blood that flows in your veins comes from the crowned heads of the world. You have been delicately nutured. Your childhood was spent between the breasts of an Egyptian queen. How can you think of a union with this base-born vagabond, whose father reeks of insect powder? She was cradled in the left ear of some mangy mongrel and earns her blood by interpretive dancing. Remember that the ballet, at least, is patronized by royalty, but that your ill-begotten paramour moves her lascivious body to the vulgar and cacophanous strains of Stravinsky and Darius Milhaud."

In vain is the pleading of the prince and futile are his arguments inspired by love for the little dancer. The tale is an old one and though often told it can well bear retelling when it is done with the fabulous skill of Prof. Heckler's troupe.

Follows the banishment from the kingdom; the young prince and his inamorata, accompanied only by a friend of his youth, flee. In the beginning, love makes all hardships into adventures, but as time passes the flighty Flearette, wearies of her royal lover's constancy, and he becomes the victim of her capriciousness. He bears his humble role bravely until the day when he accidentally discovers his light-o'-love in the arms of his friend. (Reinhardt has produced nothing like it).

We have seen the role of the prince interpreted by Moissi, John Barrymore, Emil Jannings, and Walter Hampden, but never in our thirty-three years as a dramatic critic have these old eyes been so bedimmed with dew as when the just sting of vengeance strikes the base betrayers of royal confidence.

Broken-hearted, the prince seeks to return to his native land, but unfortunately, on the very border of his country, he falls into the hands of a flea trainer. He is thenceforth compelled to act in the ow and ignoble company of a travelling circus and constantly mocked by his fellow actors for his claim to royal lineage. These benighted rascals would insist upon playfully referring to him as Mike Romanoff.

The only possible stricture I can make is one of managerial policy . . . With so much of our native talent joblessly pounding the pavement of Broadway, it is a great pity that the entire cast is of foreign origin.

MUSIC

"With a hot-cha-cha and a boop-boopa-doop."

THE FINE ITALIAN HAND

By IRVING KOLODIN

The decision, but recently announced, of Arturo Toscanini definitely to participate in the 1933 Baireuth festival during July and August cannot fail to leave somewhat aghast those who fancied that he could not avoid improving the opportunity, so easily to hand, to rebuke Frau Hitler and his lads for their current hysteria of Jew-baiting. "Il Re Arturo" (as he is known to his disciples) or less intimately, "Il Maestro", had been placed very neatly in a spot that seemed to defy merely a graceful exit; a group of American conductors (all of them Jewish and not one born here) had, on April 2nd, made public a letter on which his name was prominently placed—a letter protesting against the Nazi's "persecution of their colleagues," asking, in both the holy names of Art and Freedom, that it cease. The Nazis retaliated, two days later, by barring the signers, their records, their arrangements and their compositions, if any, from the Reich. Barring them, that is, except for the man they urgently need to keep the *Wagnerfest* out of the red, though his name was, by his own request, placed first on the manifesto.

Now, I for one make no pretense of concealing my complete bewilderment with all this. But from the confusion emerge two impressions: first, that "Il Re Maestro" doesn't give a twist of his little moustache for all of his fellow-musicians, and second, that the Hitler boys are completely at loose ends about what course they really want to pursue.

Obviously, the second conclusion is no province of a music critic; but, of the first, it is conceivable that he may be duty-bound to speak. Something may be gained, initially, by examining the past actions of the man we are concerned with. The incident in Bologna, in May 1931 is well known—Toscanini's refusal to perform or allow anyone else to perform the Fascist hymn "Giovinezza" at a memorial concert he was announced to conduct in honor of his deceased teacher Martucci; the physial attack upon Toscanini by the ardent youth of Bologna when he arrived at the hall; the subsequent cancellation of the concert; the wrath of Mussolini; the internment of Toscanini following the revocation of his passport; his subsequent martyrdom before being released. And the generous action of Koussevitzky who refused to conduct two concerts for which he had contracted in Milan, the similar action of Gabrilowitsch toward an engagement in Rome, in protest against the absurd treatment of their colleague.

This would constitute a sufficiently strong indebtedness on the part of Toscanini toward his fellows to make a gesture in kind by him now a matter of simple retribution. But to this it should be added that later in the same year, Toscanini left Baireuth "disgusted, embittered." And, to continue with his own words "I went there with the feeling of one approaching a sanctuary. I came back with the feeling of one departing from a banal theatre." It can be seen how consistently "Il Maestro" has maintained his position.

Yet the present situation is not to which it is necessary to apply the measuring-rod of past obligations or commitments. Consider that Wilhelm Fuertwaengler, who enjoys the protection and encouragement of the Nazis, openly and strenuously objected to their Aryan misadventures when that course was plainly a dangerous one for him. Certainly to Bruno Walter, Toscanini's co-worker as conductor of the Philharmonic Symphony Orchestra, there was more support than this due. Even if "Il Re Arturo" felt that sympathy for Otto Klemperer or Fritz Busch (a Sozial Demokrat, incidentally, and not a Jew) was no matter for him to meddle with, the treatment of Walker was distinctly a personal concern to one who shares his advantages in New York (though not the $2000 a concert for thirty concerts, the Toscanini fee). And to travel to Baireuth to conduct the works of a man who, as a revolutionary wrote the great bulk of his work in exile, is merely the last word in a circle of nonsense.

No, the question is essentially one of more than personal obligations or prejudices, more than merely a matter of ignoring the existence of other artists in an incomprehensible allegiance to his own inclinations. Toscanini is the one man who might have commanded international attention by a strong and challenging action, who might have bestowed a few uncomfortable moments upon Adolph, through Frau Winifred Wagner, Hitler's "bethrothed." Once again an artist has had an opportunity to present his credentials before the world as a man conscious of his social setting and the implications thereof; and once again he has shrunken away from the responsibility, costumed in the shabby cloak of his "dignity."

STOKOWSKI CONDUCTING HIS AUDIENCE

MUSIC

"Who?"
"Me?"

DOWN MEMORY LANE

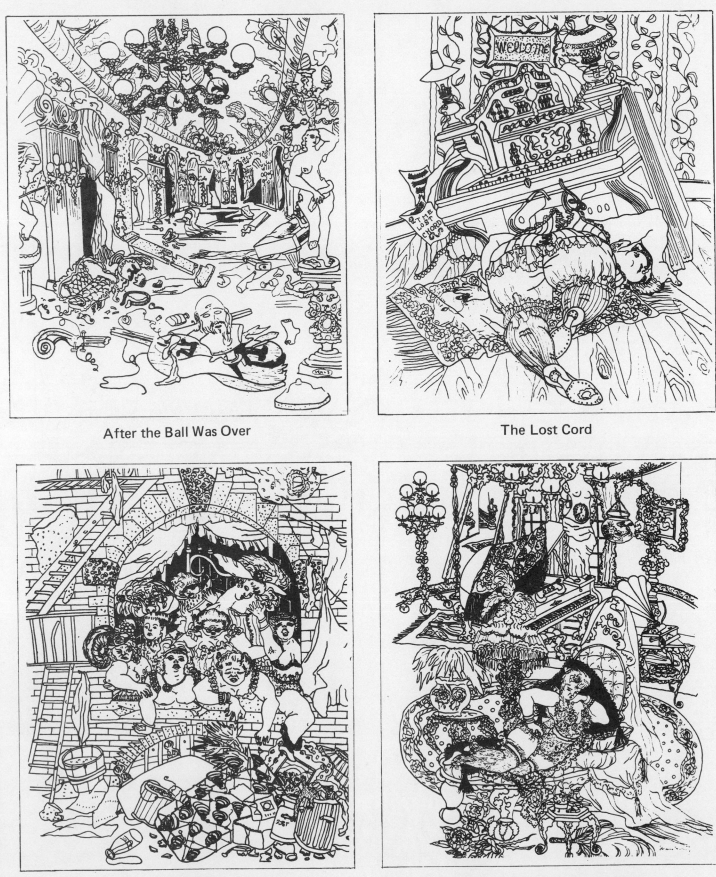

After the Ball Was Over

The Lost Cord

In the Good Old Summer Time

Only a Bird in a Gilded Cage

MODERN ART

WILD LIFE

"I wonder what became of Rockwell Kent!"

TOWN AND COUNTRY

TRINITY CHURCHYARD IN NEW YORK

CONEY ISLAND

UGH!

"Are you one of those who will be getting away from it all?"

MORE TOWN

MORE COUNTRY

OFF TO THE COLONY

PICTURESQUE AMERICA

HOLLYWOOD NUMBER

ON JULY 18, 1933, *Americana* sent out a press release announcing that Nathanael West would be joining the staff and would edit a special Hollywood issue. West had just sold his second novel, *Miss Lonelyhearts*, and moved to Hollywood, where his sister and brother-in-law, Laura and S. J. Perelman, had been working as film writers.

Segments of West's first novel, *The Dream Life of Balso Snell*, reappeared in the August and September issues of King's humor magazine, and the story "Business Deal" for the October issue is his first use of Hollywood material in his fiction. For the Hollywood number West also reprinted Perelman's classic "Scenario," which had appeared the previous February in *Contact*. Like so many transplanted East Coast writers, West in 1933 regarded Hollywood as an exotic and lucrative "colony." A new element, boredom, dominates his last novel, *The Day of the Locust*, written three years later. He writes of a young studio artist living among the bitter, betrayed people who have decided "the sun is a joke." The artist is at work on a largely conceptual canvas called "The Burning of Los Angeles." West's eye for Hollywood architecture illuminates the book, as in the final scene when he imagines working on his picture during a riot, "modeling the tongues of fire so that they licked even more avidly at a Corinthian column that held up the palmleaf roof of a nutburger stand." His vision closely paralleled the comic gifts of King and Disraeli, and it is sad that their collaboration ended here, with *Americana*'s Hollywood Number.

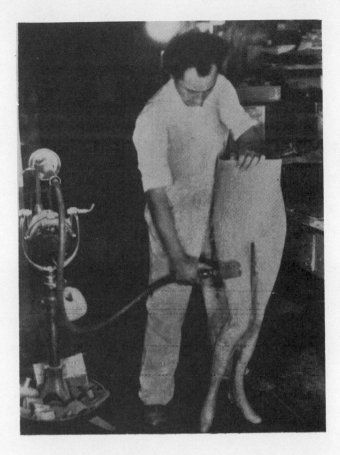

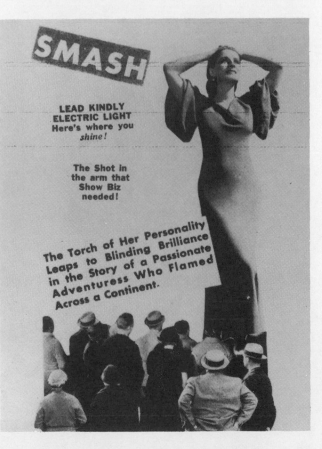

SMASH

LEAD KINDLY ELECTRIC LIGHT Here's where you *shine!*

The Shot in the arm that Show Biz needed!

The Torch of Her Personality Leaps to Blinding Brilliance in the Story of a Passionate Adventuress Who Flamed Across a Continent.

CASTING

DISRAELI

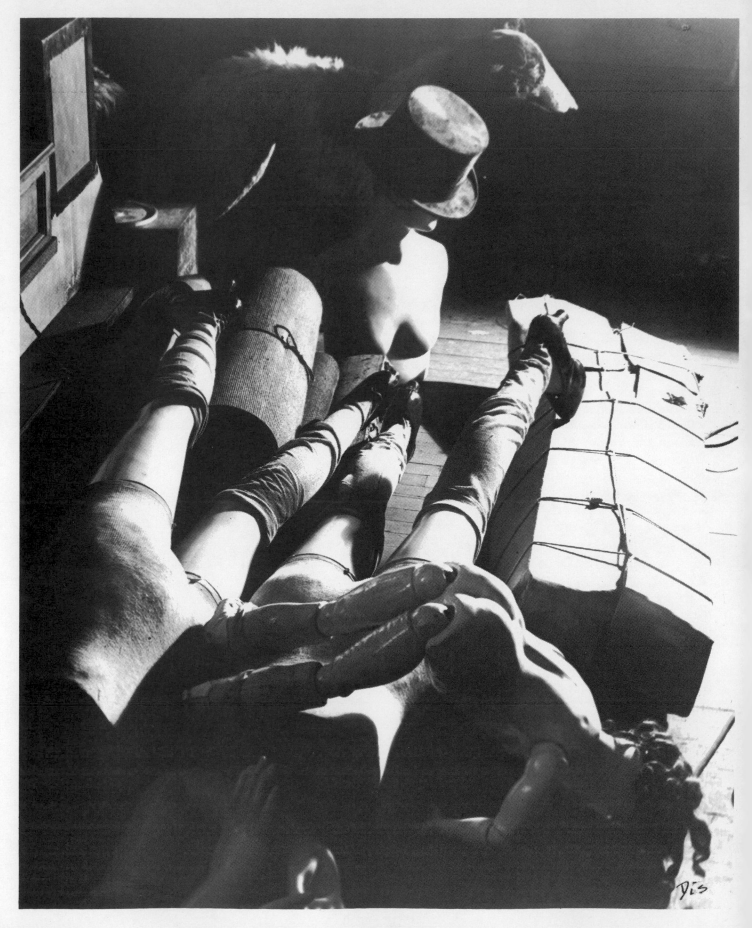

Where are the stars of yesteryear?

SCENARIO

By S. J. PERELMAN

Fade in, exterior long shot, grassy knoll. Above the scene the thundering measures of Von Suppe's "Light Cavalry Overture." Austerlitz? The Plains of Abraham? Vicksburg? The Little Big Horn? Cambrai? Steady on, old son; it is Yorktown. Under a blood-red setting sun yon proud crest is Cornwallis. Blood and ouns, proud sirrah, dost brush so lightly past an exciseman of the Crown? Lady Rotogravure's powdered shoulders shrank from the highwayman's caress; what, Jermyn, footpads on Hounslow Heath? A certain party in the D.A.'s office will hear of this, you bastard. There was a silken insolence in his smile as he drew the greatcoat about his face, and levelled his shooting-iron at her dainty puss. Leave go that lady or I'll smear ya. No quarter, eh? Me, whose ancestors scuttled stately India merchantmen of their comfits and silken stuffs and careened their piratical crafts in the Dry Tortugas to carouse with bumboat-women till the cock crew? Yuh'll buy my booze or I'll give you a handful of clouds. Me, whose ancestors rode with Yancy, Jeb Stuart, and Joe Johnston through the dusty bottoms of the Chickamauga? Oceans of love but not one cent for tribute. Make a heel out of a guy whose grandsire, Olaf Hasholem, swapped powder and ball with the murderous Sioux through the wheels of a Conestoga wagon? Who mined the yellow dirt with Sutter and slapped nuggets across the rude bars of Leadville and Goldfields? One side, damn your black hide, suh, or ah'll send one mo' dirty Litvok to the boneyard. It's right up the exhibitor's alley, Mr. Biberman, and you got to hand it to them on a platter steaming hot. I know, Stanley, but let's look at this thing reasonable; we been showing the public Folly Larrabee's drawers two years and they been cooling off. Jeez Crize—it's a hisTORical drama, Mr. Biberman, it'll blow 'em outa the back of the houses, it's the greatest thing in the industry, it's dynamite! Pardon me, officer, is that General Washington? Bless yez little heart, mum, and who may yez be, savin' yer prisince? Honest old Brigid the apple-woman of Trinity, is it? How dégagé he sits on his charger, flicking an infinitesimal speck of ash from his plum-coloured waistcoat! Gentlemen, I give you Martha Custis, hetman of the Don Cossacks, her features etched with the fragile beauty of a cameo. And I walked right in on her

Spanish Fly
Barrymore

Praying Mantis
De Mille

Earwig Gable

Louise Dahl-Wolfe

World premiere of a million-dollar super-special

before she had a chance to pull the god-damned kimono together. But to be away from all this —to lean back puffing on one's church-warden at Mount Vernon amid the dull glint of pewter, to watch the firelight playing over polished Duncan Phyfe and Adam while faithful old Cudjo cackles his ebony features and mixes a steaming lime toddy! Tired, Roy, I'm tired, I tell you. Tired of the rain, the eternal surge of the breakers on that lagoon, the glitter of the reefs in that eternity out there. Christian! She laughed contemptuously, her voluptuous throat filling with a rising sob as she faced Davidson like a hounded animal. You drove me out of Papeete but I'll go to Thursday Island with my banjo on my knee. Yeh yeh, so what? We made FOUR pictures like that last year. Oh my God, Mr. Biberman, give me a chance, it's only a flash-back to plant that she's a woman with a past. Sixteen hundred a week I pay you to hand me back the plot of "Love's Counterfeiters" Selig made in 1912! She's who? She's what? What's the idea of her coming here? What's she trying to do, turn a production office into a whorehouse? No, Miss Reznick, tell her to wait, I'll be through in five minutes. Now get it, Mr. Biberman, it's big. You establish the long shot of the messroom and dolly behind Farnsworth till he faces Charteris. I said Sixth Rajputana Rifles and I don't want a lotta muggs paradin' around in the uniforms of the Preobazhensky Guard, y' get me? Yep, he's on a tear, those foreign directors are very temperamental, did I ever tell you about the time Lazlo Nugasi said he'd buy me a brassiere if I let him put it on? Fake it with a glass shot of Khyber Pass or maybe Eddie Bollinger's got a Dunning down the shop. Now an overhead shot of the dusty tired column filing into Sidi-bel-Abbes. Shoulder by shoulder they march in the faded blue of the Legion, fun-loving Dick and serious-minded Tom. Buddies, the greatest word in the French language, flying to the defense of each other like a homo pigeon. Greater love hat Onan. Swinging a chair into that mob of lime-juicers in the Mile End Bar in Shanghai. But came a slant-eyed Chinese adventuress, and then? Don't shoot, Butch, for Gossake! Heave 'em into the prison yard, we'll keep the screws out of the cell-block and wilderness were paradise enow. Stow the swag in Cincy, kid, and go on alone, I'm done for. Too late, old Pogo the clown stopped it in the sweetbreads. They buried him outside the town that night, a motley crew of freaks and circus people. What a sequence! Old man Klingspiel told me he bawled like a baby. Laugh, you inhuman monster they call the crowd, old Pogo lies dead with only a bareback rider's spangle to mark his grave and a seat for every child in the public schools! When tall ships shook out their plumage and raced from Salem to Hong Kong to bring back tea. Break out the Black Ball ensign, Mr. Exhibitor, there's sweet music in that ole cash-register! A double truck in every paper in town and a smashing drawing by the best artist we got, mind you. Take the kiddies to that colossal red-blooded human drama of a boy's love for his dog. This is my hunting lodge, we'll stop here and dry your things. But of course it's all right, cara mia, I'm old enough to be your father. Let me go, you beast—MOTHER! What are you doing here? I ask you confidentially, Horowitz, can't we get that dame to put on some women's clothes, a skirt or something? The fans are getting wise, all those flat-heeled shoes and men's shirts like a lumberjack. Get me Gerber in publicity, he'll dish out some crap about her happy home life. Vorkapich around the room to Dmitri's brother officers as they register consternation at the news. Good chance for some hokey bellies on comedy types. What, sir, you dare mention Alexandra Petrovna's name in a saloon? The kid takes it big and gives Diane the gloves across the pan socko. The usual satisfaction, I presume? Drawing on his gloves as a thin sneer played across his features. Yeh, a martinet and for Crisakes remember it's not a musical instrument this time. But it is madness, Serge! The best swordsman in St. Mary's parish, he weel run you through in a tweenkling! Oh darling, you can't, you can't! Her hair had become undone and he plunged his face into its fragrance, unbuckling his sabre and flinging it on the bed beside them. Hurry, even now my husband is fried to the ears in a low boozing-ken in Pokrovsky Street. Of course it was he, I'd know that lousy busby anywhere in St. Petersburg. Shoot it two ways, you can always dub it in the sound track. She shrieks or she don't shriek, what the hell difference does it make? Told me he was going to night school at the Smolny Institute, the cur. And I believed him, thought Pyotr pityingly, surveying her luscious bust with greedy eyes. Never leave me, my sweet, and then bejeezus an angle shot toward the door of the General leaning against the lintel stroking his moustache. Crouching against the wall terrified yet shining-eyed as women are when men do gallant combat. Throw him your garter, Lady Aspinwall, throw your slipper, throw your lunch but for God's sake throw something! Parry! Trust! Touché! Where are they all now, the old familiar faces? What a piece of business! Grabs a string of onions and swings himself up the balcony, fencing with the soldiers. Got you in the groin that time, General! Mine host, beaming genially, rubbing his hands and belching. Get Anderson ready with the sleigh-bells and keep that snow moving. Hit 'em all! Hotter on eighty-four, Joe Devlin! Are we up to speed? Quiet, please, we're turning! Chicago, hog-butcher to the world, yclept the Windy City. **BOOZE AND BLOOD,** he oughta know, running a drug-store eleven years on Halstead Street. You cut to the back of the Big Fellow, then three lap dissolves of the presses—give 'em that Ufa stuff, then to the street —a newsboy, insert of the front page, the L roaring by —Kerist, it's the gutsiest thing in pictures! Call you back, chief. Never mind the Hays office, this baby is censor-proof! Call you back, chief. We'll heave the telephone through the glass door and smack her in the kisser with the grapefruit, they liked it once and they'll love it twice. Call you back, chief. The gat in the mesh-bag. A symbol, get me? Now remember, staccato. . . . A bit tight, my sweet? Marrowforth teetered back and forth on his heels, his sensitive artist's fingers caressing the first edition he loved. Item, one Hawes and Curtis dress-suit, one white tie, kindly return to Mister Dreyfus in the wardrobe department. What color do I remind you of? Purple shot with pleasure, if you ask me. Do I have to work with a lot of pimply grips giving me the bird? Papa's in the doghouse and keep up the tempo of the last scene, you looked crummy in yesterday's daily. A warm, vivid and human story with just that touch of muff the fans demand. Three Hundred Titans Speed Westward as King Haakon

"... and in Bing Crosby's last letter to me ..."

Lays Egg on Shoe-String. In the freezing mists of dawn they gathered by the fuselage of their planes and gripped hands. But Rex Jennings of the shining eyes and the high heart never came back. Heinie got him over Chalons, I tell you it's murder to send a mere boy out in a crate like that! The god-damned production office on my neck all day. It's midsummer madness, Fiametta! You mustn't! I must! I want you! You want me? But I—I'm just a poor little slavey, and you—why, all life's ahead of you! Fame, the love of a good woman, children! And your music, Raoul! Excuse me, miss, are you Fiametta Desplains? I am Yankel Patchouli, a solicitor. Here is my card and a smear of my recent urinalysis. Raoul! Raoul! Come quick! A million dollars! Now you can go to Paris and study your counterpoint! Damn my music, Fiametta, my happiness was in my own back yard all the time and I was, how you say it, one blind fool. The gingham dress and half-parted lips leaning on a broom. But why are you looking at me in that strange way, Tony? . . . Tony! I'm afraid of you! Oh . . . You utter contemptible despicable CAD. He got up nursing his jaw. Spew out your poison, you rat. You didn't know she was the morganatic wife of Prince Rupprecht, did you? That her affairs with men were the talk of Vienna, did you? That—Vanya, is this true? Get out. *Get out.* GET OUT! Oh, mumsey, I want to die. That hooker's gotta lay off that booze, Mr. Metz, once more she comes on the set stinking and I take the next boat back to Buda-Pesth. But in a great tangled garden sits a forlorn tragic-eyed figure; the face a mask of carved ivory, the woman nobody knows—Tilly Bergstrom. What lies behind her shattered romance with Grant Snavely, idol of American flapperhood? Turn 'em over, you punks, I'll stay on this set till I get it right. The jig is up, long live the jig—ring out the old, ring in the new. For love belongs to everyone, the best things in life are free.

LEADING MEN

JAPAN

RUSSIA

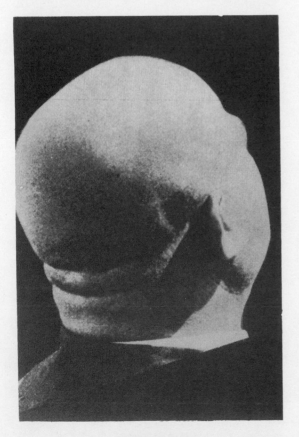

GERMANY

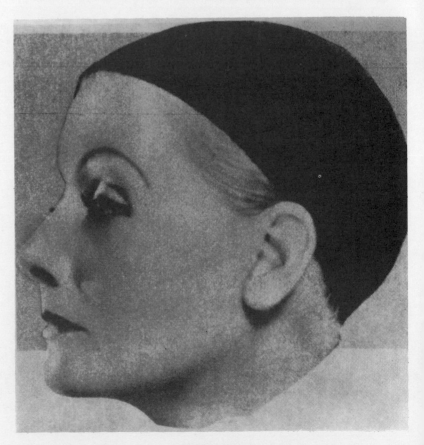

AMERICA

223

HOLLYWOOD ARCHITECTURE

Hot Dog Stand

Dairy

Movie Theatre

Comfort Station

CECIL B. DE MILLE PLANS
NEW SUMMER HOME

Servant's Quarters

Garage

Outhouse

Woodshed

BUSINESS DEAL

By NATHANAEL WEST

For an hour after his barber left him, Mr. Eugene Klingspiel, West Coast head of Gargantual Pictures, worked ceaselessly. First he read *The Hollywood Reporter, Variety,* and *The Film Daily.* Then he measured out two spoonfuls of bicarbonate and lay down on the couch to make decisions. Before long Mr. Klingspiel had fallen into what he called a gentle reverie. He saw Gargantual Pictures swallowing its competitors like a boa-constrictor, engulfing whole amusement chains. In a delicious half-doze, he found himself wondering whether to absorb Balaban & Katz; but finding no use for Katz, he absorbed only Balaban, and turned next to Spyros Skouras and his seven brothers. Perhaps at the outset he ought to absorb only three of them. But which three? The three in the middle or two on one end and one on the other? Finally he arranged the eight Skourases into a squad of tin soldiers and executed five at random. The repeated buzz of the dictograph cut short his delicious sport. He flipped the switch irritably.

"Who is it?"

"Hwonh hwonh hwonh hwonh hwonh."

"I'll see them later," said Mr. Klingspiel. "Send in Charlie Baer."

"Hwonh-hwonh."

He lit a cigar, turned his back on the door, and set his features into a scowl which would have done credit to a Japanese print. No punk kid two years out of Columbia College could hold *him* up for money, no matter how many hit pictures he'd written. After a dignified interval, he swung around. Charlie Baer, moon-faced and unconcerned, was staring out of another window with his back to Mr. Klingspiel.

"Well, Charlie." Mr. Klingspiel controlled his irritation at this breach of respect and essayed a kindly smile. "I sent for you yesterday."

"Aha." Charlie stared placidly at Mr. Klingspiel. His dewy innocence was positively revolting.

"My girl phoned you at the Writers' Building, but they said you were working with Roy Zinsser in Malibu." Mr. Klingspiel cleared his throat. Maybe a good joke would clear the atmosphere. "Vas you dere, Sharlie?" He regretted it immediately; Charlie's frigid stare made the remark almost indelicate. So this weasel thinks he can hijack me, Mr. Klingspiel reflected angrily.

"Charlie," he began, screwing his face into an expression of deep disapproval, "I dint like that last script. It lacked guts. It dint have the most important thing a good comedy script should have."

"What's that?" asked Charlie without curiosity.

"Spontinuity," replied Mr. Klingspiel gravely. "Now if I were you, Charlie, I'd take that idea home and maul it around in your mind over-night."

"Oke," said Charlie, reaching for his hat.

"Oh, just one more thing." Mr. Klingspiel made believe he was consulting some papers. "You expire on the fifteenth, am I right?"

"Yep."

"Well, Charlie, I'm gonna lay it on the line. You did some great pictures. I'm gonna extend you another year, but this time at two-fifty a week." Charlie's eyes remained fixed on his. Mr. Klingspiel was radiant. "In other words, double what you're getting now. How's that?"

"No good," said Charlie. "Five hundred a week or I don't work."

"Listen to me," said Klingspiel. "Answer me one thing. How many fellers do you know twenty-three years old that make two-fifty a week?"

"I've got to think about my old age," said Charlie.

"When I was twenty-three," went on Mr. Klingspiel, well into his Plowboy-to-President mood, "what was I? A green kid working for buttons. All I could afford was a bowl of milk and crackers. You don't know how lucky you are."

"Yes, I do," said Charlie. "I once tried a bowl of milk and crackers."

"Yes—this is Metro Meyer Goldwyn speaking."

"Now, look here, Charlie," said Mr. Klingspiel patiently, "why don't you get wise to yourself? A single man like you in no time could bank——"

"Five hundred," interrupted Charlie bovinely. Mr. Klingspiel drummed softly on his desk.

"Listen, Charlie," he said after a moment, "let me tell you a story. It's a story about Adolph Rubens, the man who founded this great organization." Charlie's eyes drooped slightly. "Just picture to yourself that there ain't no Hollywood, no film business, nothing. It's twenty-eight years ago. A poor little furrier named Adolph Rubens is walking down a windy street in St. Louis. He's a little man, Charlie, but he's a fighter. He's cold and hungry, but in that man's brain is a dream. Everybody laughs at him and calls it Rubens' Folly, but he don't care. Why? Because in his brain he sees a picture of a mighty amusement ennaprise bringing entertainment and education to millions of people from coast to coast. And today that dream has come true. This ain't a business, Charlie; it's a monument created by the public to Adolph Rubens' ideals, and we're building all the time."

"Five hundred dollars or I stop building," said Charlie in the same metallic tone.

"Charlie," said Mr. Klingspiel after a moment, "I want you to do something. Come here. Not there—come around this side of the desk." He arose. "Now you sit down in my chair. That's right." He encircled the desk, then turned and faced Charlie. "Now put yourself in my place. You're Eugene Klingspiel, the head of Gargantual Pictures. You got a payroll of three hundred and forty-six thousand dollars a week. You got stars that are draining you dry. Nobody goes to pictures any more, they stay home and listen to the radio. You got a lot of dead-wood writers drawing their check like clockwork every Wednesday. Now, in walks a fella named Charlie Baer. He don't want much, only the shirt off your back. And what do you say to him?" He gripped the edges of the desk and stared into Charlie's face.

"Five hundred dollars or I turn in my badge," droned Charlie. Mr. Klingspiel's eyes glittered. The mongoose sat comfortably and waited for the cobra to strike again.

"Now let's be sensible," said Mr. Klingspiel. "I could buy four gagmen for what I'm paying you." Charles stood up. "But I'll tell you what I'm gonna do. Three hundred——"

"Mr. Klingspiel," said Charlie, "there's something I ought to tell you. Metro——"

"What?" Mr. Klingspiel quivered like a stag.

"Metro offered me four-fifty yesterday."

"So that's it," said Mr. Klingspiel. "That's how much loyalty you got. We pick you up from the gutter——four-twenty-five!"

"Listen," said Charlie coldly, "I'm a scenario-writer, not a peddler." He put on his hat.

"Just a minute," said Mr. Klingspiel. His face cleared suddenly. "I'm gonna teach that Metro crowd a lesson. Beginning the fifteenth Charlie Baer gets five hundred dollars a week from Gargantual—and Eugene Klingspiel *personally* guarantees that! And any time you got any problems I want you to come—— Where you going?"

"Lunch," said Charlie, and smiled briefly. "You know, just a bowl of milk and crackers."

Mr. Klingspiel belched and grabbed for the bicarbonate.

"Aw, boloney! What's Marlene Dietrich got that Greta Garbo ain't got?"

The sad case of the humorous magazines*

BY ALEXANDER KING

BEING FUNNY FOR MONEY.

Although Americans have an excellent sense of humor and the wisecrack is much more typical of us than — let us say — the Negro spiritual, one looks in vain through our comic publications for some veracious echo of our native wit. There is just one minor, local exception to this state of affairs in the pages of *The New Yorker*. I say "minor" and "local" though I realize that is so doing I am practically knocking at the door of the "Go-Climb-a-Tree Department."

The history of the comic magazine in this country shows a constantly growing estrangement between editorial office and public. The streets, the clubs, the highways, and general stores of the land have echoed for years to the fine, salty, cynical comments of unpaid humorists, while their professional brethren were devising cross-word puzzles for a handful of old subscribers.

This has not always been so. The comic weeklies played an enormously important part in the development of our national *mores,* and not half a century ago they were still potent factors in politics. There was a time when quacks and demagogues trembled before them lest they be laughed out of office.

Approximately twenty-five humorous publications had failed in the United States before the emergence of *Puck* in 1877. This was the first comic magazine with any sort of virility. It was published by Keppler and Schwartzman, who were printing a German magazine under the same name, for which Keppler was the principal illustrator. The American *Puck* was destined to live for forty years under various editors but during the period of its greatest success, Nathan Straus, Jr. was its guiding spirit.

In the early days its contents were distinctly eclectic, like all publications of that period, but within a few years it had found an original and satisfactory policy. Its pages were hospitable to men of considerable humorous talent, and unlike its bankrupt forerunners it disdained to imitate *Punch*. Among its contributors were Bret Harte, H. C. Bunner, F. Opper, and in later years, Hy Mayer, James Huneker, Ralph Barton, Edgar Saltus, and Marius de Zayas. It is worth remembering that all conservative and knowing publishers had agreed from the very beginning that this venture was destined to be short-lived.

When *Puck* was four years old and managing very nicely, a certain Ike Gregory, one-time editor of the Elmira (N.Y.) *Gazette,* launched a humorous weekly of a frankly Republican tinge, called *Judge*. In his first editorial Ike announced that he had started his paper for fun and that the acquisition of money was not his object. For many prosperous years this dictum was certainly violated but the present incumbents of his office can justly claim that his original intentions are now finally fulfilled.

In the year 1883, a young artist, John Ames Mitchell, but recently returned from Paris, decided to print a new comic weekly although his friend, Henry Holt, an experienced publisher, advised him very strongly against it. Young Mitchell, having been thoroughly cautioned gathered a staff, and with the help of Edward S. Martin, released the first issue of *Life,* a magazine which is now half a century old. It was difficult sailing at the start but after an investment of only eleven thousand dollars he managed to make his infant self-supporting.

THE HEYDAY OF "LIFE" AND "JUDGE"

For many years these three magazines had the humorous publication field to themselves and it is interesting to observe the causes of their rise and decline. *Puck's* flavor at the start was pointedly satirical and its humor concerned itself with the average daily occurrences of life. It carried drama and book criticisms and unlike its predecessors it did not attempt to impress potential customers and critics in England. It definitely aimed to please the well-bred American reader, employed artists and writers who were funny rather than famous — men since become famous — and gave to its pages an effect of unusual variety.

Life and *Judge* frankly imitated this policy but sought at the same time to develop distinct characteristics of their own. Early in its career *Life* adopted a strong anti-vivisection attitude and gained thereby many sentimental readers. It started a fresh air fund for poor children and contributions poured in to send unfortunate city waifs on summer vacations. These apparently irrelevant features in a humorous publication were logical at a time when people of quality and purchasing power considered joke papers a little undignified. By these strategems *Life* became a magazine for the home, where, previously, the humorous publications had been confined largely to barber shops and men's clubs.

Incidentally, *Life*'s pages became increasingly crowded with stories and pictures of cats and dogs. Artists who specialized in animals and in children flocked to its offices, and *Life* gave full play to such men as Dickey, Crosby, Rannels, Herford, and Harrison Cady. But their greatest contributor and eventual owner was Charles Dana Gibson. Mr. Gibson, a draughtsman of unusual skill, had discovered that by lengthening the distance between eyebrows and eyelash he could create a new type of particularly haughty pure-looking Anglo-Saxon female. This lady gained enor-

*From the December 1933 issue of Vanity Fair

mous popularity, and the Gibson Girl remained the rage for a decade. Her image graced college dormitories, and the dens of male bachelors were furnished with leather pillows on which her aristocratic profile had been burnt with hot needle. American women consciously tried to resemble her, and succeeded. She became the ideal of a nation.

The whole school of illustrators thrived on this invention. James Montgomery Flagg, Clarence Underwood, and Coles Phillips borrowed, for a time at least, both technique and subject from Gibson but none of them ever approached him in talent.

A G.O.P. CHAMPION.

Meanwhile *Judge* devoted itself to its Republican heroes. Garfield, McKinley, and Roosevelt marched triumphantly and militantly through its pages and the artists — Nast, Zimmerman, Outcault, Dirks, and Flagg — made both themselves and the magazine famous. The popular scandals and causes of the day were courageously and sometimes brilliantly satirized. They were valiant sponsors of the full dinner pail. The old numbers of this publication are infinitely superior to the more recent issues because they reflect the true spirit of their time.

Eventually these magazines began to have an evil influence on each other. At the turn of the century *Puck* began publishing lachrymose double pages about home and mother. Later on they poked fun at *Life*'s anti-vivisection campaign. They hired many of the most expensive literary and artistic lights from their competitors and from other magazines.

In 1918 *Puck* became a monthly and shortly afterward expired. Its epitaph is a list of its contributors during that last year. They were Nell Brinkley, K. C. B., George Jean Nathan, Alan Dale, Carolyn Wells, Rea Irvin, and Bruno Lessing. At the height of their success, these three magazines employed huge quantities of superfluous, expensive, and unamusing people. They became arrogant, conservative, and stuffy, and losing complete sight of their prime functions as humorous weeklies, they standardized their material until it lost all contact with the turbulent life and reality about them. They had become bloated and devitalized. The earlier comic magazines, *Figaro, Lantern, The Wasp, The Mule, Reveille, O. K.,* and the old *Vanity Fair* (a weekly — modeled on *Punch* — which began publication in 1861 and ceased in 1865; its chief claim to fame rested in the fact that Artemus Ward, then the reigning humorist of the day, was its editor), had failed for lack of variety, from a scarcity of contributions, and because they were hopelessly under-staffed. They had no advertising and their sole revenue came from sluggish and tardy subscribers. *Puck, Life,* and *Judge* remedied some of these difficulties but their weekly payrolls eventually consumed all their profits.

Fifteen years ago, *Life* and *Judge* each had a sale of over 300,000 copies per week. They have since become monthlies and their combined circulation is less than this figure per month.

These magazines, which had for several decades a monopoly of the humor of America, have lately made determined efforts to attune themselves to the temper of the changing times. In one of the pre-election numbers an editor of *Judge* boldly asserted his intention to vote for Norman Thomas. The contents of the magazine, however, showed that the publication was dying, in excellent taste, of a lack of vitality. It was not Socialism but humor and satire that was required.

A magazine of this type is only as good as its editor or sponsor, and for years no single individual was able to carry out his ideas without the meddlesome coöperation of timid and unimaginative committees. Robert Benchley, Norman Anthony, Don Herold, S. J. Perelman, or Pare Lorentz, all able contributors, could each perhaps have done a reasonable job of editing. In conjunction with four or six committeemen, their capacities became diluted into a thin broth.

There is some tradition in America that a humorous magazine is not a very suitable vehicle for advertising. But it is possible nowadays, as has been demonstrated with *Americana*, to publish a magazine at so low a production cost that a sizeable profit can be made on sales alone. It is not my intention to gloss over the shortcomings of *Americana* in this general appraisal of the humorous publications. Its failings are many and obvious. But it was conceived and launched during the depression with practically no financial resources. Most of the work was done by two people, who, incidentally, earned their livelihood at something else. But it has not turned its back on the grotesque political and economic scene and has chosen to employ the camera with intelligence and humor. It has frequently shrieked when a whisper would have been adequate and is often raucous beyond good taste. But its policy, that many things are evil and all things are funny, has relevance — and never more than today.

AND "THE NEW YORKER."

As a demonstration of the accuracy of the foregoing conclusions, take the extraordinary and well-merited success of *The New Yorker*. In back of that magazine one feels the creative intelligence of its editor, Harold Ross.

Ross, a real phenomenon in the American publishing field, was a shiftless newspaper reporter, temporarily covering the water front for the *San Francisco Examiner*, when we entered the war. He enlisted, of course, and discovered on his arrival in France that there was great need for some sort of informal publication. He consulted the proper authorities and within a few weeks he published that sprightly and amusing sheet, the *Stars and Stripes*.

Upon his return to the States, Ross entered the magazine field, became editor of *Judge*, but finding the atmosphere hopelessly stultifying, he decided to start a venture of his own. His new magazine, *The New Yorker*, is simply a continuation, in a new environment, of the *Stars and Stripes*.

Ross, born in Colorado, in manner and appearance anything but a New Yorker, edits, with the assistance of two other country bumpkins, the completely inexperienced Messrs. White and Thurber, the most sophisticated journal in the land. The three guiding spirits of this sophisticated weekly move in an editorial atmosphere which is a cross-section between a psychopathic ward and a tramp steamer. Their office is noted for its lugubrious air and it seems inconceivable that a lively magazine can originate there.

Ross set a new course in the field of humorous publications. He discovered the unique talents of White, Thurber, and the early Peter Arno. Unlike the other magazines, the prose of *The New Yorker* became significant despite the excellence of the pictorial material, and although Ross aimed definitely at class circulation, he created a popular success.

He knew how to flatter his readers into a mood of worldliness and made his publication into a hall-mark for smart city life. All its imitators are now defunct and it alone survives and holds its readers from year to year. It is often shallow, frequently monotonous, but always at least partly amusing. It has reduced the technical originality of its draughtsmen to three or four easily recognizable patterns and permitted the unpardonable decline of Peter Arno to his present pathetic state, but it has re-discovered the single line gag, and managed to be consistently original in presenting obscure and amusing aspects of New York. It deals with personalities irreverently yet preserves enough tact to maintain the good will of its advertisers. It carries a sufficient ballast of boring material to present an air of stability to the serious business man, and is, on the other hand, sly enough to make typists and bank clerks consider themselves intellectuals — a sensation which no other magazine is offering for fifteen cents.

The one outstanding success, unparalleled in the annals of the humorous publication field, is, of course, *Ballyhoo*. Norman Anthony, an erstwhile editor of both *Life* and *Judge* and temporarily out of a job, persuaded that canny promoter Mr. George Delacorte to back this morbid venture. It seemed obvious to the publisher that such a magazine, destined to offend potential advertisers, was bound to fail, and with considerable misgivings, he launched the first issue. Within six months *Ballyhoo* had a circulation of 1,700,000.

Ballyhoo also failed to hold its public and this chiefly due to the fact that it relied for its success almost entirely on satirizing national advertising. When once the well-known slogans had been sufficiently burlesqued, its editors to fill the pages had to descend to bawdy versions of the usual *Life* and *Judge* jokes. The keynote of *Ballyhoo*'s uniqueness is now gone, but after two years, it still sells 300,000 copies a month.

SELECTED LIST OF CONTRIBUTORS

Biographical notes in the list, especially for more familiar contributors, focus on their activities at the time their work appeared in *Americana*.

EUGÈNE ATGET (1856–1927) was a French photographer whose principal subject matter was Paris. His work was made known to connoisseurs in the 1930s through the American photographer Berenice Abbott (1898–   ), who had preserved his negatives.

PEGGY BACON (1895–   ) ranked among the country's leading printmakers. Her drypoints were widely exhibited, and her drawings of cats made her sought after as an illustrator for any book concerning that animal. An author of delightful children's books, including the doggerel classic *The Ballad of Tangle Street* (1929), she published in 1931 a collection of poems, *Animosities*, illustrated with drawings Edmund Wilson called "as compact as medals of Pisanello, as clear as tiny plates by Callot." Bacon won a Guggenheim in 1933 to complete the caricatures published the following year in *Off With Their Heads*.

HOWARD V. BAER (1906–   ) published regularly in *Esquire* after it began in 1933. He became known as an illustrator of children's books. In 1957 he would publish *Now This, Now That*, a pictorial essay on relativity for the pre-schooler.

KENNETH BURKE (1893–   ), music critic for *Dial* in the 1920s, published *Towards a Better Life: Being a Series of Epistles, or Declamations* in 1932. In 1933 he attacked the effects of capitalism on art, but his views were considered too biased to be acceptable to the dogmatic left. He became an eminent essayist and teacher of literature.

Peggy Bacon *Self Portrait*

Miguel Covarrubias *Self Portrait*

VICTOR CANDELL (1903–1977), a Hungarian-born painter, came to the United States when he was eighteen. Largely self-taught, he had recently returned from Paris in 1932. In the late 1930s he would spend several months painting among the coal miners in Scranton, and in 1939 he received a commission for a mural at the Iraq pavilion of the World's Fair. Candell had his first one-man show at the Mortimer Brandt Gallery in 1943. After 1946 he taught at the Brooklyn Museum and in the 1950s at the Provincetown Workshop. His later paintings were dynamic abstracts of jagged, colliding forms.

WILLIAM COTTON (1880–1958) made portraits before selling his pastel caricatures to Frank Crowninshield at *Vanity Fair* in 1931. He later drew several covers for the *New Yorker*. His comedy, *The Bride the Sun Shines On*, was mounted by the New York Repertory Theatre in 1931.

MIGUEL COVARRUBIAS (1904–57), born of a wealthy family in Mexico City, had become famous for his caricatures as a teenager. He arrived in New York when he was nineteen and immediately found a market in *Vanity Fair*. His first book came out when he was twenty-one, followed by *Negro Drawings* in 1927. In 1932 he was producing an appealing series for *Vanity Fair* called "Impossible Interviews." He would later turn to the serious study of Indian art of the Americas, publishing *Mexico South* in 1946 and *Eagle, Jaguar and Serpent* in 1950.

E.E. Cummings *Self Portrait*

PERCY CROSBY (1891–1964) drew the popular syndicated strip "Skippy." In 1932 he published *Vets and Wets, Let's Go*, pursuing a parallel career as a polemicist. His foes were Prohibition, Roosevelt, labor unions, and communists.

E. E. CUMMINGS (1894–1962), poet and author of the novel *The Enormous Room*, had his play *Him* produced at the Provincetown Playhouse in 1928 (a run of 27 performances). In 1931, he visited Russia briefly, and in 1932 published *CIOPW*, a collection of his work in charcoal, ink, oil, pastel, and watercolor.

LOUISE DAHL-WOLFE (1895–   ) opened her own photographic studio in Manhattan in 1933; the photograph in *Americana* was one of the first she ever published, along with *The Smokey Mountaineer*, which was given a spread opposite an Erskine Caldwell story in the November '33 *Vanity Fair*. In 1936 she was appointed staff photographer of *Harper's Bazaar* where one of her most celebrated color photographs, a cover of Lauren Bacall, appeared in 1943.

ADOLF DEHN (1895–1968) emerged as a master printmaker in the late 1920s after a long apprenticeship in Europe. His lithographs were included in the annual "Fifty Best Prints" shows that circulated in America in the early Depression years. In 1931 he was a contributing editor of *New Masses*, and in the spring of 1932 had a show at the Weyhe Gallery. He spent that summer at his parents' farm in Waterville, Minnesota, the subject of several of his prints.

LAWRENCE DENNIS (1893–1977), was an Atlanta-born Harvard graduate who became the country's leading intellectual fascist. He had retired from the Foreign Service, where he had served in Central America, to join a private investment firm. In 1932 he was writing on Latin American issues for *The Nation* and *The New Republic*, and published his first major book, *Is Capitalism Doomed?* the same year. In 1936, with *The Coming American Fascism*, Dennis predicted the coming war.

FRANK DI GIOIA (1900–   ) exhibited his tempera and ink drawings of New York's Little Italy at the Marie Harriman Gallery in December 1933. The son of a Neopolitan sculptor, Di Gioia had one-man shows of works depicting the Italian quarter into the 1960s.

ROBERT DISRAELI (1903–   ), born in Cologne, was educated in New York City. From 1934–38 he made candid photographs of writers and publishers for his regular feature in the *Saturday Review of Literature*, "News Pictures of the Month." His works were also included in the *U.S. Camera* annuals of the 1930s. Disraeli's 1933 book, *Seeing the Unseen*, introducing young people to the microscope, was still in print thirty years later. He also wrote *Here Comes the Mail* (1939) and *Uncle Sam's Treasury* (1941) before his long career as an educational filmmaker. Exhibitions of his works were held at the Marcuse Pfeifer Gallery in 1982 and the Photofind Gallery, Woodstock, N.Y., in 1983.

MURIEL DRAPER (1886–1952) had published her memoirs *Music at Midnight* in 1929, the same year she wrote an introduction for Taylor Gordon's *Born to Be*, a book (illustrated by Covarrubias) which emerged from the Harlem Renaissance. Her neighbor in 1932, Edmund Wilson, described her "ready instinct for understanding people." Her son was the dancer Paul Draper.

LOUIS G. FERSTADT (1900–1954) had come to New York from Chicago on a scholarship to the Art Students League. In 1931, finding it difficult to sell his works, he invited the public to visit his Union Square studio to buy his drawings. Later that year his painting *Friendship*, of two female nudes, was removed from a show at the Hotel Marguery when a resident complained. After supervising a WPA mural project, he remained active in the Mural Artists Guild.

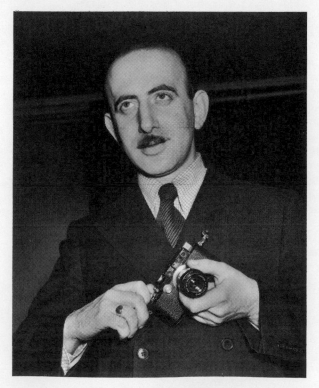

Robert Disraeli

George Grosz by Miguel Covarrubias

ALEXANDER KING (1899–1965) was among the best known book illustrators in New York when he launched *Americana*. He had illustrated deluxe editions of DeFoe and Dickens, Swift and Smollett, Boccaccio and Dostoevsky. Under the pseudonym of Charles D. Young, he had published a translation of Ovid in 1930. Soon after *Americana* foundered, he wrote a profile of Rose O'Neill, the originator of the Kewpie doll, which was published in the *New Yorker* in November 1934. He then became managing editor of *Stage* and religious editor of *Life*. His children's story, *The Great Kerplunk*, illustrated by his son Robin, was published in 1962; during this period his memoirs became best sellers.

IRVING KOLODIN (1908–　　) was music critic for the *Brooklyn Eagle* for almost a year before joining the *New York Sun* early in 1932 as assistant critic. In 1936 Kolodin published his first book — *The Metropolitan Opera: 1883–1935. The Kingdom of Swing* followed in 1939. After serving in World War II, Kolodin would become the *Sun's* principal music critic. In 1950 he joined the staff of the *Saturday Review of Literature*. Later he joined the Juilliard School of Music faculty.

GEORGE GROSZ (1893–1959), a few months before he arrived in America in 1932, showed about a dozen works in the 12th annual watercolor exhibition in Chicago. Nearly all were sold, and *Married Couple*, the drawing singled out by Jonas Lie as an example of art that would have an unhealthy influence if Grosz were invited to teach at the Art Students League, was purchased by the famous film director Josef von Sternberg. Grosz had published his last series of drawings with the Malik Verlag in Berlin in 1930, *The New Face of the Ruling Class*, and a series for Bruno Cassirer's press, *Love Above Everything*; these drawings lacked the political content of his former work.

PERKINS HARNLY (1901–　　) was born on a cattle ranch in Ogalalla, Nebraska. At the time of his work for *Americana*, Harnly's architectural fantasies were inspired by his two years in residence at lavish Carabas Castle, the Connecticut home of Rose O'Neill (the hospitable designer of the Kewpie doll had invited him to tea). Alexander King first bought Harnly's drawing of a corseted house and promoted his work, arranging an exhibition at the Julien Levy Galleries in late 1933. In 1942 Harnly went to Hollywood, where he worked on the props for *Portrait of Dorian Gray*. Employed most of his later life as a cafeteria counterman, Harnly exhibited 29 paintings at the National Museum of American Art in 1981.

ALBERT HIRSCHFELD (1903–　　), now America's foremost caricaturist, studied at the Art Students League and the Académie Julian in Paris. He contributed to *New Masses* in the 1920s and published his first caricature in the *New York Times* in 1925. During 1927–28 he worked in Russia, and traveled to Bali in 1931. His theatrical caricatures, running in the *Times* for more than 50 years, have been collected in a number of anthologies, including *Show Business is No Business* (1951), *The World of Hirschfeld* (1970), and *Hirschfeld by Hirschfeld* (1979). He has also completed several mural commissions.

Al Hirschfeld *Self Portrait*

ALEXANDER Z. KRUSE (1890–1972), painter and printmaker, was art critic for the *Brooklyn Eagle*. In 1932 he exhibited in the "Self-Portraits by Etchers" show at the Philadelphia Art Alliance.

ALFRED KUBIN (1877–1959) was a renowned Austrian artist and illustrator, whose ominous drawings were featured regularly in *Simplicissimus*. His autobiography and his "fantastic novel" of 1909, *Die andere Seite*, were widely read by artists.

SIDNEY LAZARUS (1912–1973) was on a scholarship at the Art Students League when he submitted a drawing to the *Americana* art contest and remained to work with King through the run of the magazine. A protégé of Jean Charlot, Lazarus had his first one-man show at age 20 at Julien Levy's and another drawings show in June 1938. He worked for the Metropolitan Museum of Art in the early 1940s, then settled in Newburgh, N.Y., from 1946–57. A prolific writer, Lazarus continued to develop an art based on inner vision, calling his works "primagraphs," or records of thought.

JOSE CLEMENTE OROZCO (1883–1949), Mexican muralist and draftsman, spent the summer of 1932 in Spain. He returned to the United States in the fall to resume work on a large mural in the reserve book room of the Baker Memorial Library at Dartmouth. A major monograph on his art with 230 reproductions came out in New York that December.

S. J. PERELMAN (1904–79), the leading American humorist of his generation, was hired by Norman Anthony as an artist and writer for *Judge* in 1925. He published his initial piece in the *New Yorker* in 1931. The first of his many books, *Dawn Ginsburgh's Revenge*, came out in 1929, shortly before he went to Hollywood. Perelman then wrote the scripts for the Marx Brothers' *Monkey Business* and *Horse Feathers* and in 1932 was producing material for Broadway revues. His profile of Jimmy Durante ran in *Life* in 1933.

Gilbert Seldes by E.E. Cummings

MARY PETTY (1899–1976) had her first cartoon in the *New Yorker* in October 1927. She drew 38 covers for the magazine during her career. Her collection of cartoons, *This Petty Pace*, was published with an introduction by James Thurber in 1945.

GILBERT SELDES (1893–1970) was brought up with his brother in a utopian community in New Jersey founded by his Russian immigrant father, an anarchist, who published his own view of history in 1932. Seldes worked on *Collier's* before joining *Dial*, where he was managing editor from 1920–23. After *The Seven Lively Arts*, his first book, appeared in 1924, Seldes wrote for all the major magazines, seeking out the original and mocking whatever struck him as false or pretentious. In 1937 Seldes became director of television for CBS, and from 1950–63 he was a professor at the Annenberg School of Communications at the University of Pennsylvania.

J.S. Perelman by Al Hirschfeld

JOHN SLOAN (1871–1951) resigned his presidency of the Art Students League on March 31, 1932, when the board of the art school voted against his inviting George Grosz to teach there in the summer session. After lively student protests, the board relented, but Sloan did not return to the faculty until 1935. He taught during part of the summer of 1932 in Woodstock at the school established there by the sculptor Archipenko. According to the *New York Times*, he met Grosz for the first time on October 4 at the tea held in honor of the German artist by *Americana*.

WILLIAM STEIG (1907–   ) was a staff cartoonist on the *New Yorker* in 1932 when he sold a few drawings to *Americana*. About this time he introduced his engaging series "Small Fry." Steig has watercolors and sculpture in various museum collections, and since *Sylvester and the Magic Pebble* (1969), his children's books generally win awards in that field for the year they appear. His collections include *About People* (1939), *The Lonely Ones* (1942), *Faces* (1949), *Till Death Do Us Part* (1947), *Agony in the Kindergarten* (1949), *The Rejected Lovers* (1951), *Dreams of Glory* (1953), *Male/Female* (1971), and *Drawings* (1979).

Lynd Ward Self Portrait

John Sloan by Robert Disraeli

LYND WARD (1905–   ) published the first of his evocative novels in wood engravings, *God's Man*, in 1929. *Mad Man's Drum* followed in 1930. Some of his highly acclaimed illustrations for Goethe's *Faust* were reproduced in *Vanity Fair* in 1931. The following year Ward's *Wild Pilgrimage* appeared, and he illustrated a new edition of Charles Reade's *The Cloister and the Hearth*. *Prelude to a Million Years* was published in 1933 by Equinox Cooperative Press, founded by Ward and several colleagues the previous year. In 1935 Ward drew a biography in lithographs of John Reed for Equinox called *One of Us*. *Song Without Words* (1936) and *Vertigo* (1937) were his last works in the demanding field of narrative printmaking, in which he surpassed Frans Masereel, the Belgian artist whose art had inspired him. His "woodcut novels" were collected and documented in *Storyteller Without Words: The Wood Engravings of Lynd Ward* in 1974. The first major survey of his work was organized by George Barringer at Lauinger Library, Georgetown University, in 1983.

M. R. WERNER (1897–1981) had published biographies of P. T. Barnum, Brigham Young, and William Jennings Bryan, when he visited Russia in 1930. That same year his book *Orderly* appeared. A close friend of E. E. Cummings, Werner later became an associate editor at *Sports Illustrated*.

NATHANAEL WEST (1903–1940) joined William Carlos Williams in 1931 as co-editor of *Contact*; the first of four issues appeared in February 1932, the same month King founded *Americana*. *Contact* attempted "to cut a trail through the American jungle without the use of a European compass," a purpose enough akin to *Americana*'s to induce West to join King as co-editor in the summer of 1933. West, however, had moved to California and participated chiefly in the Hollywood number of October 1933.

ART YOUNG (1866–1943) was the country's best-loved and, perhaps, most effective political cartoonist when King announced that his drawings would appear in *Americana*. Praising his 1928 autobiography *On My Way*, Edmund Wilson said Young had accomplished a rare and difficult feat in modern America: "...at the cost of popular success, and even of regular employment, he has managed to keep the shape of his personality and the quality of his intelligence." In 1933 *Art Young's Inferno* appeared, and in January of 1934 his works were exhibited at Delphic Studios.

Art Young by Lynd Ward

Several major contributors—Arroyito, Paul Busch, Majeska, Willi Noell, Nordley, Herman Post, and Charles Silver—do not appear in the list above because of insufficient biographical information. They are listed with other contributors in the index to works included in this anthology. Others who signed work appearing in *Americana* which is not included in the present volume are: Berenice Abbott, Alain, Cotbin, B. Darwin, Jr., Louis M. Eilshemius, Emanuel Eisenberg, Eugene Fitsch, Don Gordon, B. G. Guerney, Wynn Holcomb, Terry Jackson, Otto Kleist, Ernest Lorsy, Dorothy McKay, Joseph Mitchell, Albert Muldavin, H. Owen, Clarence T. Raymond, Clinton Seymour, Cleon Throckmorton, James Thurber, and Dudley Warren.

FURTHER READING

Appelbaum, Stanley. *Simplicissimus*. New York, Dover, 1975.

Becker, Stephen. *Comic Art in America*. New York, Simon and Schuster, 1959.

Feaver, William, and Ann Gould. *Masters of Caricature*. Alfred A. Knopf, 1981.

Grosz, George. *George Grosz: An Autobiography*. Trans. Nora Hodges. New York, An Imago Imprint/Macmillan, 1983.

_____. "Briefe aus Amerika," *Kunst und Künstler 31* (August, September, and December 1932), 273–8, 317–22, 433–43.

Heller, Steven. *Man Bites Man*. New York, A & W Publishers, 1981.

Hirschfeld, Albert. *The World of Hirschfeld*. New York, Harry N. Abrams, 1970; new edition, *Hirschfeld's World*. New York, Harry N. Abrams, 1981.

Horn, Maurice, and Richard E. Marschall, eds., *The World Encyclopedia of Cartoons*. New York, Gale Research Co., 1980.

King, Alexander. *Mine Enemy Grows Older*. New York, Simon and Schuster, 1958.

_____. *May This House Be Safe From Tigers*. New York, Simon and Schuster, 1960.

_____. *I Should Have Kissed Her More*. New York, Simon and Schuster, 1961.

_____. *Is There a Life After Birth?* New York, Simon and Schuster, 1963.

_____. *Rich Man, Poor Man, Freud and Fruit*. New York, Simon and Schuster, 1965.

Lewis, Beth Irwin. *George Grosz: Art and Politics in the Weimar Republic*. Madison, Milwaukee, and London, University of Wisconsin Press, 1971.

Murrell, William. *A History of American Graphic Humor*, Vol. II (1865–1938). New York, Cooper Square Publishers, 1967.

O'Sullivan, Judith. *The Art of the Comic Strip*. Catalogue of an exhibition held at the University of Maryland Art Gallery, College Park, Maryland, April 1–May 9, 1971.

Shikes, Ralph E. *The Indignant Eye: The Artist as Social Critic in Prints and Drawings from the Fifteenth Century to Picasso*. Boston, Beacon Press, 1969.

_____ and Steven Heller. *The Art of Satire*. New York, Pratt Graphics Center/Horizon Press, 1984.

Simplicissimus. Catalogue of an exhibition held at the Haus der Kunst, Munich, Nov. 19, 1977–Jan. 15, 1978.

Ward, Lynd. *Storyteller Without Words: The Wood Engravings of Lynd Ward*. New York, Harry N. Abrams, 1974.

Wilson, Edmund. *The Thirties*. Ed. and with an introduction by Leon Edel. New York, Farrar, Straus and Giroux, 1980.

_____. *The Shores of Light*. New York, Farrar, Straus and Giroux, 1952.

INDEX OF CONTRIBUTORS

Some names in the list may be pseudonyms for Alexander King or others. Parenthetical numbers following page references in the index refer to the *Americana* issue in which the contribution appeared. Issues are numbered according to the following code, based on the complete numbered set at the Library of Congress, Washington, D.C.:

1 February 1932 (Vol. I, No. 1)
2 April 1932 (Vol. I, No. 2)
3 May 1932 (Vol. I, No. 3)
4 July 1932 (Vol. I, No. 4)
5 November 1932 (New Series, Vol. I, No. 1)
6 December 1932 (n.s. Vol. I, No. 2)
7 January 1933 (n.s. Vol. I, No. 3)
8 February 1933 (n.s. Vol. I, No. 4)
9 March 1933 (n.s. Vol. I, No. 5)
10 April 1933 (n.s. Vol. I, No. 6)
11 May 1933 (n.s. Vol. I, No. 7)
12 June 1933 (n.s. Vol. I, No. 8)
13 July 1933 (n.s. Vol. I, No. 9)
14 August 1933 (n.s. Vol. I, No. 10)
15 September 1933 (n.s. Vol. I, No. 11)
16 October 1933 (n.s. Vol. I, No. 12)
17 November 1933 (n.s. Vol. II, No. 1)